In the Company

o f

Manatees

In the Company

of

Manatees

A Tribute

Barbara Sleeper

PHOTOGRAPHS BY

Jeff Foott

Three Rivers Press
NEW YORK

To my parents, Norma and Bill Sleeper, and my three exuberant manatee-loving kids, Kelly, David, and Josh. Thank you for your humor and support throughout this project.

— BARBARA SLEEPER

To Mr. and Mrs. W. O. Foott, thanks for the encouragement.

— JEFF FOOTT

Grateful acknowledgment is made to Dave Barry for permission to reprint excerpts from his April 26, 1998, column in *The Miami Herald*. Reprinted by permission of Dave Barry.

The sidebar quotes on pages 115, 147, 148, 155, 156, 169, and 171 are reprinted from *Biodiversity* with permission. Copyright © 1988 by the National Academy of Sciences. Courtesy the National Academy Press, Washington, D.C.

Published by Three Rivers Press,
201 East 50th Street, New York, New York 10022. Member of the Crown Publishing Group
Random House, Inc. New York, Toronto, London, Sydney, Auckland
www.randomhouse.com
Three Rivers Press is a registered trademark of Random House, Inc.
Printed in China

DESIGN BY LYNNE AMFT

Library of Congress Cataloging-in-Publication Data
In the Company of Manatees: A Tribute / by Barbara Sleeper; photographs by Jeff Foott.
Includes bibliographical references and index. 1. Manatees. I. Title.
QL737.S63S57   1998
599.55—dc21   99-11971

ISBN 0-609-80331-X
10 9 8 7 6 5 4 3 2 1
First Edition

Acknowledgments

✿

The authors wish to thank the following people and organizations for their invaluable assistance on this book:

WAYNE HARTLEY, ranger, Blue Spring State Park

LYNN LEFEBVRE, ROBERT BONDE, CATHY BECK, JIM REID, GALEN RATHBUN, and THOMAS O'SHEA, U.S. Geological Survey, Sirenia Project, Biological Resources Division

JAMES "BUDDY" POWELL, DANIEL HARTMAN, THOMAS PITCHFORD, SCOTT WRIGHT, BRUCE ACKERMAN, MONICA ROSS, KAREN STEIDINGER, LAYNE BOLAN, and DAVID ARNOLD, Florida Department of Environmental Protection

JUDITH VALLEE, NANCY SADUSKY, CONNIE GRAHAM, PAT ROSE, Save the Manatee Club

GARY STOLZ, refuge manager, U.S. Fish and Wildlife Service; affiliate professor, University of Idaho

RANDALL REEVES, Chair: IUCN/SSC Cetacean Specialist Group

JOHN E. REYNOLDS III, Eckerd College

DARYL P. DOMNING, Howard University, editor of *Sirenews*

DANIEL ODELL, SeaWorld Orlando

GREGORY BOSSART, Miami Seaquarium

EDMUND and LAURA GERSTEIN, Florida Atlantic University

SKIP SNOW, National Park Service, Everglades National Park

TED ONDLER, U.S. Fish and Wildlife Service, Chassahowitzka National Wildlife Refuge

ROBERT TURNER, U.S. Fish and Wildlife Service, Jacksonville, Florida

TRACY BRYANT, Florida Power and Light Company

ROSS WILCOX, Florida Atlantic University

EDWARD SEEC, Florida Department of Transportation

WINDLAND RICE, DAWN SCHLUTZ, and SANDRA MORLEY, Jeff Foott Productions

JONI PRADED and STAFF, *Animals* magazine, Boston, Massachusetts

ROBERT RATTNER, Wildlife Preservation Trust International

Homosassa Springs State Wildlife Park/SUSAN DOUGHERTY

Blue Spring State Park

Crystal River National Wildlife Refuge

Lowry Park Zoo

South Florida Museum, Bishop Planetarium and Parker Manatee Aquarium

PING and SHARON ALBERDI, Crystal River

Aqua Terra Sea Kayaks

Special thanks go to WILLIAM SLEEPER for helpful computer research assistance throughout the project; to BOB CITRON for the financial support and childcare needed to write this book; to BOB BONDE, GARY STOLZ, LYNN LEFEBVRE, and Save the Manatee Club for their helpful reviews and suggestions; to GALEN RATHBUN for nearly a quarter-century of inspiration to write about manatees; to TOM O'SHEA and WAYNE HARTLEY for sharing the playful, nurturing, and mischievous world of manatees; to MIKE KONECNY, who made it possible to view manatees from the air in Belize; to editor JESSICA SCHULTE, without whose patience and talents this book would never have been published; to the late BRANDT AYMAR for his friendship and enthusiasm for a manatee book; to designer LYNNE AMFT, whose artistic talents are expressed in the beautiful layout of this book; to JOY SIKORSKI, production manager and manatee enthusiast; to MARK MCCAUSLIN, whose devotion to this project and manatees is supreme; and to the faith and goodwill of Crown Publishers, who made this project possible.

Contents

❧

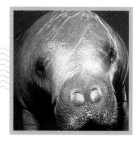

Preface

༄

For the Love of Manatees

"ASSESSING THE OUTLOOK FOR MANATEES AS PESSIMISTIC or optimistic probably has more to do with the personality of the assessor than the outlook," says Lynn Lefebvre, project leader of the U.S. Geological Survey Sirenia Project. "I find some cause for optimism because manatees are one of the most loved species in the world, they are highly adaptable to human-altered environments, and they seem to like us despite all that we've done to them and their habitat."

The tremendous mobilization now under way to protect Florida's state marine mammal is as much a heartwarming story about people as it is about manatees. It involves a remarkable network of government agencies, private corporations, conservation groups, and research facilities, all peopled by an army of devoted individuals, both paid and volunteer, who are working together for a single cause—to save the manatees. It is an uplifting story of cooperation between people of all ages, back-

PRECEDING PAGE:

Florida manatees can be found wherever water temperatures are mild and seagrass beds abundant—primarily in the slow-moving rivers, lakes, canals, estuaries, and saltwater bays of Florida and southern Georgia.

grounds, and disciplines who share the same passion—a love for one of nature's gentlest, most inquisitive, and most harmless of creatures.

As *Homo sapiens* continue to launch rockets into space, build inhabited space stations, encircle the globe with a web of telecommunications satellites, and search our galaxy for extraterrestrial life, we will be lucky indeed if we ever find a more interesting "alien" than the manatee. As an endangered ambassador from another age and time, this living fossil has much to teach us. Swimming and grazing as they do in the quiet waterways of Florida, manatees create a tangible, thought-provoking juxtaposition between our ancient mysterious past, the high-tech present, and our unknown future on planet Earth.

The Manatee as Teacher

Through the ages, people have exploited manatees for their meat, oil, and hides and for their carvable, ivorylike bones. They have worn manatee ear bones as charms in the hope of improving human hearing, and they have applied or ingested other manatee body parts as "medicinal" cures that are as dubious as they are bizarre. Manatees have been enlisted as underwater lawn mowers to battle invasive alien weeds, and they have helped to keep mosquito populations in check by eating the insect's breeding habitats.

But, finally, the most significant role of this endangered species may be that of teacher. As a bigger-than-life "poster child" for conservation and environmental protection, this lovable, elliptical marine mammal makes a bold conservation statement.

As we strive to understand why manatees are endangered, and how we can best protect them, manatees teach us the most valuable lesson of all—that for better or worse, from the microscopic to the macroscopic, from manatee to microbe, we are all intricately interconnected with one another in a very fragile, symbiotic dance of life. By recklessly destroying one species after another as we fell forests, drain wetlands, and carve up coastal shorelines, not only do we jeopardize an ancient creature as remarkable as the manatee, but we ultimately threaten ourselves.

Like peaceful aliens from another time and place, manatees mean no harm. These curious, gentle giants with hound-dog faces and pudgy proportions—comical caricatures of the legendary mermaids—have endeared themselves to people young and old. They are evolutionary markers from an age long past, when life, and those living it, moved at a much simpler, slower pace.

As such, manatees bring out the best and worst in human nature. A few sad individuals find it cruelly amusing to abuse an animal that is so big yet so helpless. A few more view manatees as a hindrance to high-speed boat thrills and continued waterfront development. Others see them only as "sea cows," an easily conquered source of floating protein, leather, and oil.

Luckily for the Florida manatee, the growing majority of people find that manatees have much to teach us about a calmer, quieter, gentler way of life. Like charismatic canaries in an aquatic coal mine, manatees patrol our shallow coastal waterways. Their very presence is an affirmation of the health of their aquatic environment—and of our own. As long as they are okay, we are okay. Manatees are a relic species whose evolutionary path is etched across millions of years. They are a tangible link to our biological as well as spiritual past.

Maybe their appeal simply boils down to manatee envy, the desire to exchange our high-tech terrestrial life of stress and pressure (not to mention gravity) for the three-dimensional freedom and joyful buoyancy of life spent in water—on slow-motion manatee time.

But since this isn't possible, at the very least we can work hard to preserve an ancient animal whose only reason for being on an endangered species list is us.

BELOW: *Florida's Timucuan and Seminole Indians once hunted manatees from canoes and called their prey "big beavers" because of their huge flattened tails.*

Introduction to the Manatee

A BLANKET OF MIST CURLS OVER FLORIDA'S PLACID ST. Johns River at dawn. Mullet and tilapia bubble and jump at the surface. A great blue heron stands knee-deep at the shoreline, intently poised to strike. From its riverside perch, an osprey gracefully swoops down to the water's surface for a swift talon-snatch plunder of fish. Red-shouldered hawks, a glimpse of river otter, alligators, egrets, and live oaks stretching their majestic, moss-draped branches over the dark tannin-colored water enhance this primordial scene.

I had traveled to Orlando, Florida—not to visit the Magic Kingdom or Universal Studios, but instead to head northeast out of town, to Blue Spring State Park, the site of this bucolic scene. The sole purpose of my journey was to catch a rare glimpse of an animal that has survived an evolutionary history spanning more than 50 million years, a mammal closer in time to the dinosaur than to humans—the manatee.

PRECEDING PAGE:
The manatee's serene, slow-paced lifestyle is well suited for Florida's limestone springs where saltwater fish mix freely with freshwater species, and Pleistocene fossils often rest in piles at the bottom of the deepest subterranean caverns.

ABOVE: *A great blue heron patiently awaits its next aquatic meal while striking a statuesque pose near Blue Spring State Park.*

ABOVE RIGHT: *Two manatees float in the misty, primordial setting of Blue Spring State Park. From November to March, Florida manatees seek the warmth of limestone springs and power plant effluents to pass the cold fall and winter months.*

RIGHT: *A great egret skims the surface of the St. Johns River to catch an unsuspecting fish. Wildlife views such as this make Florida a nature lover's paradise.*

LEFT: *Emersed in duck weed, an American alligator basks in the warm Florida sun. These large reptiles peacefully share habitat with manatees at Blue Spring State Park.*

BELOW LEFT: *Manatees share space with a variety of aquatic creatures, including salt- and freshwater fish, green and loggerhead sea turtles, and Florida red-bellied turtles, pictured here sunbathing on a log.*

ABOVE: *An energetic river otter bobs to the surface to breathe. Its quick movements are in sharp contrast to those of the slow-motion manatees, with which it shares water habitat.*

Without contest, the manatee is North America's most unusual marine mammal. Averaging 10 feet in length and half a ton or more in weight, the Florida manatee (a subspecies of the West Indian manatee) is one of the largest inshore mammals associated with our continent.

"They are huge," says New Smyrna Beach resident Robert Mattson. "They've got a back about the size of a refrigerator."

The largest Florida manatee on record measured 13 feet in length; the heaviest was over 3,500 pounds. And females tend to be larger than males of the same age. Disarmingly docile, these gentle giants have been described as a cuddlier version of a walrus—minus the tusks.

Built like pudgy submarines, with pinprick eyes, valved nostrils, broad spoon-shaped tails, and flippers with fingernails, manatees look as if they were designed by Disney. These misproportioned "mermaids" are covered with thick grayish brown skin mottled with dark green algae above, sometimes barnacles, and a sparse scattering of long individual hairs—the perfect camouflage for such a hefty, water-loving creature.

Search the surface for them, and the mesmerizing interplay of dappled sunlight and shadow, filtered and distorted through water, creates an optical illusion. Under such conditions, without the benefit of polarized sunglasses to improve visibility into water, a manatee's body outline seems to break up and disappear, leaving the big animal nearly invisible as it floats at the surface to breathe, "walks" along the bottom of a shallow waterway with its flippers, or dozes for hours in the gentle currents.

In the United States, manatees can be found wherever water temperatures are mild and seagrass beds abundant—primarily in the slow-moving rivers, lakes, canals, estuaries, and saltwater bays of Florida and southern Georgia. During the warm summer months, individual manatees have migrated as far north as Rhode Island and as far west

RIGHT: *Florida manatees live in fresh, saline (salt), and brackish water. They move freely between these salinity extremes as long as they have periodic access to fresh drinking water, provided here by Blue Spring.*

OPPOSITE: *The manatee's large size, docile behavior, and diet of aquatic plants led people to nickname them sea cows. They have also been described as big baked potatoes with flat frying pans for tails, walruses without tusks, and floating "sea sofas."*

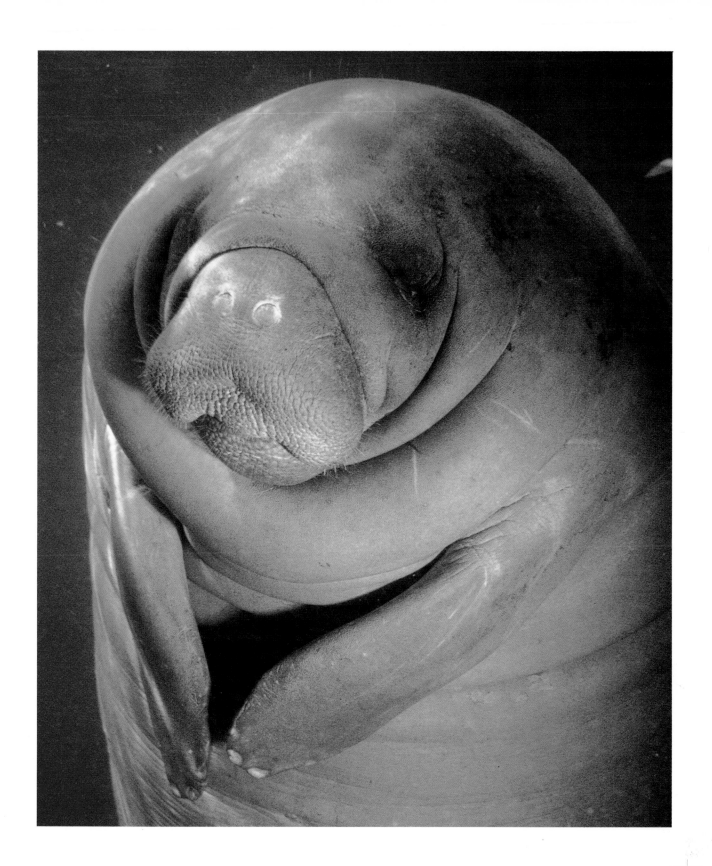

Introduction to the Manatee

as Texas. But as fall approaches, they head for Florida's natural limestone springs, which are warmed at a constant 72 to 74 degrees Fahrenheit by geothermal groundwater—and to artificial habitats created by the warm effluvial discharge from several power-generating plants.

In fact, the manatees' diet of shallow-water plants and need for tepid water—preferably 72°F. or above—defines their habitat. Despite protection from a thick layer of skin and a modest layer of fat, manatees are highly susceptible to cold because they evolved in the tropics. The southern part of Georgia and the northern Gulf of Mexico represent a climatic barrier above which they cannot survive during a temperate winter. Prolonged exposure to cold water 68°F. and below can put the animals at risk of hypothermia and other potentially fatal health problems.

Orlando is an interesting place to begin a search for manatees. Named after Orlando Reeves, a soldier shot with an arrow by a Seminole Indian warrior in 1835, this booming metropolis is one of Florida's few inland cities. Yet this popular tourist town has 77 lakes and 56 miles of shoreline. To venture past the periphery of Orlando's commercial, billboarded heart is to trade one type of sensory overload for another—but one that can be far more memorable.

"Just beyond the concrete highways and the miles of hotels and fast-food joints," wrote author Steve Kaplan of the Orlando area, "the cypress swamps of primordial Florida still teem with wildlife and exotic vegetation. After a hard day of riding freeways, there's almost nothing more relaxing than just floating down Shingle Creek in the shade of cypress, oak and pine stands, amid the fragrance of acacia, enjoying the natural beauty of the swamp."

LEFT: *A group of manatees rests in the cathedral-like setting of Blue Spring State Park, where biologists often spy on their behavior while perched in branches overhanging the water.*

BELOW: *Like an underwater magician, a manatee appears to conduct a school of passing Crevalle Jack with its flipper.*

Florida, with its extraordinary bounty of tropical and subtropical wildlife, does seem the fitting place to search for manatees. With some 40 different species of snakes, it boasts one of the largest local serpent faunas in the world. Alligators haunt the blackwater swamps along with 100-pound alligator snappers—the world's largest freshwater turtle. The shallow creeks offer up huge salamanders, called conger eels, that grow 2 to 3 feet in length. Florida is also home to eyeless crayfish, blind white salamanders, plenty of red-bellied leeches—and frogs of every description that make the cypress swamps and hammocks resonate with their amorous spring choruses. Three-hundred-pound bull sharks the size of canoes have been spotted swimming up the Suwannee River.

Even more interesting is the fact that much of Florida rests on soluble limestone. This porous foundation provides occasional excitement when huge chunks of land suddenly fall through the roof of a collapsing underground cavern, or large bodies of water suddenly drain away. Such is life in limestone country, where sinkholes have swallowed up houses and cars, and others have spontaneously unplugged from below, leaving aquatic residents high and dry as their liquid habitat has been audibly sucked into the water table below.

"I often wonder," wrote *Natural History* author Daniel Lenihan, "if motorists nearing Orlando in the endless stream of cars heading south to Disney World have any idea that they have been passing for miles over a fantasyland that rivals any theme park."

Lenihan was referring to the maze of water-filled catacombs that snake through the limestone mantle of northern and central Florida, just beneath all things civilized. Home to strange, dark-adapted creatures, the catacombs form when rainwater filters through the topsoil and mixes with carbon dioxide from decaying organic material. This produces a mild acid solution that, over time, has dissolved the limestone into a labyrinth of underground tunnels and chambers. When the surface suddenly collapses into such a chamber, a sinkhole is formed. Filling quickly with groundwater, these gaping holes provide divers access to a wondrous subaquatic world beneath the surface.

Florida's limestone foundation has created not only magical environments for adventurous scuba divers, but also important habitats for the state's native wildlife—including manatees. The subterranean maze of interconnected chambers is filled with water under hydrostatic pressure. As ongoing erosion weakens spots in the chamber walls, the pressurized water escapes to the surface, creating an artesian spring. These effervescent, freshwater "fountains" can be found all over the state.

"The artesian, rheocrene springs that boil up and flow away as little rivers are the singular blessing of the Florida landscape," wrote naturalist Archie Carr in *A Naturalist in Florida.* In fact, several of these thermally warmed springs, such as Blue Spring, and those in Crystal River, provide the critical winter habitat that makes it possible for the otherwise tropical West Indian manatee to range as far north as Florida.

More than 300 major springs have been identified in Florida. The best known is Silver Springs, near Ocala. It forms the Oklawaha tributary, which flows into the St. Johns River. The deepest is Wakulla Springs, south of Tallahassee, which emerges from a depth of 200 feet to join the St. Marks River. Another third of Florida's springs occur

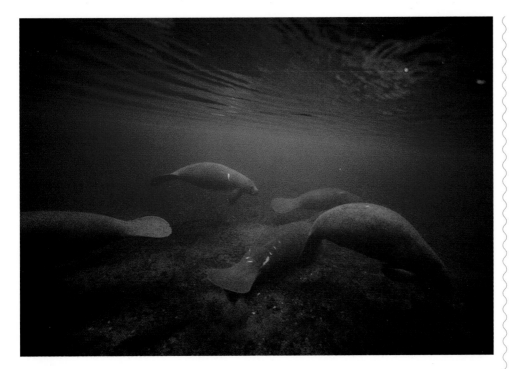

beside or within the channels of the Suwannee River and its main tributaries—used by summering manatees on the Gulf Coast.

In the deepest Florida springs, scuba divers have discovered eerie piles of alligator and turtle bones mixed with fossils of Ice Age mastodons, saber-toothed cats, and extinct camels, giant tortoises, and Pleistocene horses. Scientists estimate that the first humans reached Florida before the end of the Ice Age at least 11,000 years ago: radio-carbon dating has indicated that a skull and brain fragments discovered at Warm Mineral Springs, near Sarasota, and preserved in the highly ionized and anaerobic environment of the spring are at least 10,200 years old.

Yet manatees existed long before the first trace of humans and Ice Age animals now preserved at the bottom of Florida's mysterious springs. This is what makes them so fascinating. Not only did manatees survive when so many other prehistoric species did not, but it is still possible to see them—often in Florida's freshwater springs.

"It is always an eerie feeling to realize I may be watching a living fossil, a species in danger of joining the dinosaur and the mastodon as part of Earth's past," wrote scuba diver/author M. Timothy O'Keefe of the manatee. Ironically, Florida was discovered in 1513 by Spanish explorer Ponce de León during his quest for the mythical Fountain of Youth. It turns out that Florida's artesian springs are far more magical than Ponce de León ever dreamed. As aquatic gateways to the prehistoric past, they provide both refuge and gravesite for haunting ancient creatures—some, like the manatee, still living, the rest long extinct.

All of Florida's popular west-coast springs form streams that flow several miles directly into the Gulf of Mexico. In contrast, all of the state's major east-coast springs

"To place human evolution in a time perspective, recall that life originated on Earth several billion years ago, and that the dinosaurs became extinct around sixty-five million years ago. It is only between six and ten million years ago that our ancestors finally became distinct from the ancestor of chimps and gorillas. Hence human history constitutes only an insignificant portion of the history of life."

≋

—JARED DIAMOND, *in* The Third Chimpanzee

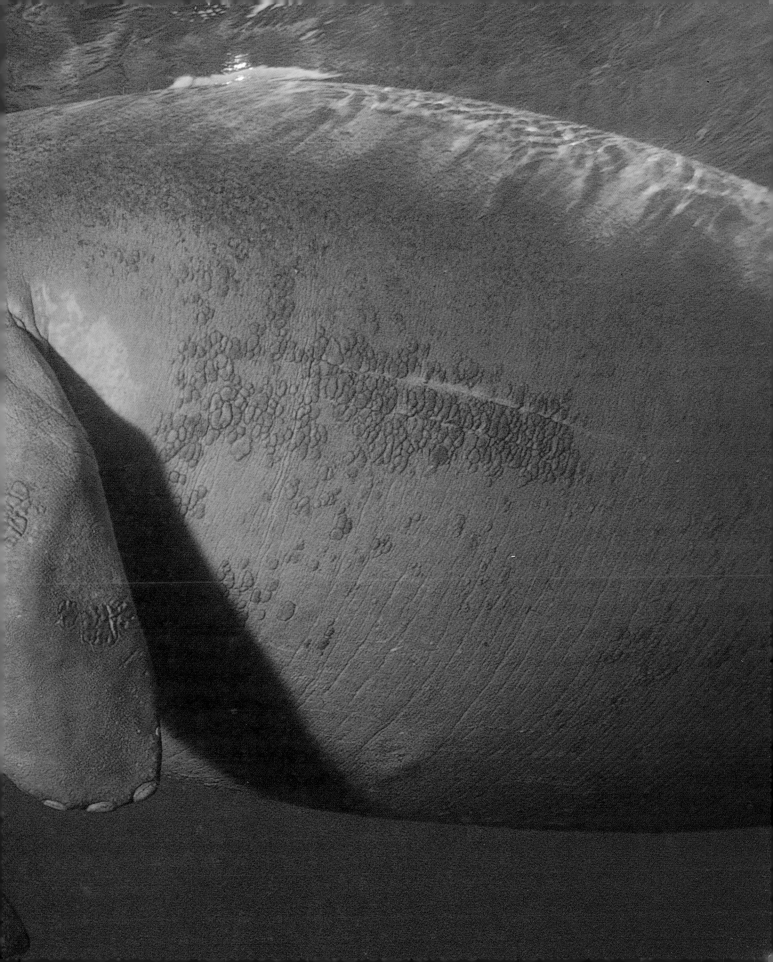

PRECEDING PAGES:
Although Florida manatees
average about a half-ton in
weight, the largest on record
weighed more than 3,500
pounds.

flow directly into the St. Johns River, not the Atlantic Ocean. Blue Spring contributes 100 million gallons a day to this river system, which begins far down the Florida peninsula on the Kissimmee Prairie and hugs the coastline for 260 miles to its mouth above Jacksonville. During spring and fall, manatees use the river to migrate along the north and central portions of Florida's east coast—the tea-colored river, once used by early explorers to access Florida's interior, falls only 20 feet during its entire course, posing no impediment to the animals' progress.

Archie Carr considered the St. Johns River an extraordinary stream, like no other in America, because of the high number of marine animals that live in the freshwater river, either permanently or seasonally. He attributed their presence to the dissolved salts flowing into the river from the artesian springs. As a result, manatees share Florida's artesian waters with the most amazing assortment of salt- and freshwater creatures, such as sea catfish, speckled sea trout, redfish, and schools of jacks and pinfish, as well as freshwater snails, crayfish, bluegill bream, longnose gars, black bass, and schools of stumpknockers. Marine species such as mullet, tarpon, and snook are also found in most of Florida's big springs, along with blue crabs, the Gulf pipefish (a straightened-out seahorse), and the hogchoker (a two-inch sole).

In my search for manatees that day, from a wooden observation platform built along Blue Spring Run, I scanned the dark surface of the tree-shaded water. Amid birdcalls and jumping fish, it was the sound of a heavy exhaled breath that caught my attention. Visually drawn to the forceful sound, I turned in time to see two large nostrils release a vaporous cloud, inhale, close, and disappear beneath the surface, leaving hardly a ripple. That was it. My first poignant glimpse of a manatee in the wild was of its nostrils and nothing more.

Now I understood why this elusive animal had evaded scientific scrutiny for so long. Difficult to see in the water due to its cryptic behavior and coloration, the manatee appeared as little more than a spindle-shaped gray shadow as it quietly resubmerged

RIGHT: *A manatee exhales a*
vaporous breath of air at Blue
Spring State Park. Like ceta-
ceans, manatees can replace up
to 90 percent of the air in their
lungs with a single breath—
humans replace only about
10 percent with each breath.

to the bottom of the run to join several other ghostly forms. In fact, so unobtrusive are the movements of these large mammals that only the subtlest of clues hint at their presence—gentle swirls at the water's surface, a mysterious mud trail, or the rounded tip of a nose poking through the surface to breathe.

And yet, submerged at the bottom of Blue Spring Run, surrounded by a quiet, cathedral-like setting of lush vegetation, the manatee had a haunting presence. Here was the mammal that had survived the vicissitudes of evolutionary time, to outlive mastodons, giant sloths, and saber-toothed tigers, even Ice Age people. And here it was, dozing serenely in the middle of the Space Age—in the protected, palm- and live-oak-canopied waters of a Florida state park.

There is definitely something appealing about the doleful, slow-motion manatee. These roly-poly mammals reach right out and grab your heart. Described by some as big, smiling potatoes with flippers, manatees are the closest incarnation to an aquatic Pillsbury Doughboy. In fact, ad agencies would be hard pressed to invent a more anthropomorphic character. The manatee's somewhat comical appearance matches its affable personality. A gentler, more good-natured creature can hardly be imagined. Innocent, inquisitive, and often playful, manatees do not have a mean or aggressive bone in their portly bodies.

"Perhaps it is the irony that the most peaceful and harmless of animals is dying the most painful and violent deaths that has stirred the public's sympathy," says Judith Vallee, executive director of Florida's Save the Manatee Club. "The manatee has captured the hearts and imaginations of people from all over the globe—inspiring them to write poetry, sing songs, paint pictures, and rally to the aid of this defenseless and lovable gentle giant."

Watching the graceful, unobtrusive movements of the manatees gathered at Blue Spring Run that day, I began to understand why.

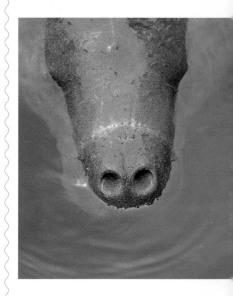

BELOW: *A manatee opens its valved nostrils to breathe at the surface. Like a floating iceberg, the majority of the manatee's enormous body remains hidden just below the waterline.*

LEFT: *Having evolved over millions of years, and survived, manatees are considered relic species, or living fossils. Here a manatee takes up a particularly prehistoric pose at the bottom of Blue Spring Run.*

Myths, Legends, and Folklore

ONCE CONSIDERED A FISH, LATER THOUGHT TO BE A WHALE, then mistakenly described as "half-human," the Sirenia (a group of aquatic mammals consisting of manatees, dugongs, and the extinct Steller's sea cow) have had a confused identity. With thick, wrinkled skin like that of an elephant, a paddle-shaped tail reminiscent of a beaver's, a bulbous walrus-shaped body, and a small head with tiny eyes and big droopy lips, the manatee has inspired both legend and controversy.

On January 9, 1493, off the coast of Hispaniola (the modern-day Dominican Republic and Haiti), Christopher Columbus saw what he thought were three "mermaids" *(serenas)* lift their heads out of the water near the Rio Yaque del Norte. In his journal he wrote, "They are not so beautiful as they are painted; though to some extent they have the form of a human face." His journal entry is believed to be the first documented sighting by a European of manatees in the New World.

PRECEDING PAGE: *A manatee rests on the tip of its tail at Crystal River.*

RIGHT AND OPPOSITE: *Manatees are perfectly adapted for life in a liquid. Their streamlined body shape enables them to move gracefully through the water.*

BELOW: *A Florida manatee lifts its head out of the water at SeaWorld Orlando in a pose reminiscent of a portly mermaid. Sea-weary sailors mistook manatees for mermaids more than 500 years ago, hence their Latin name,* Sirenia, *after Homer's tale of bewitching sirens.*

M y t h s ,   L e g e n d s ,   a n d   F o l k l o r e

RIGHT: *Manatees have been described as "overstuffed sausages with heads and tails." Yet, such portly proportions do not prevent them from suffering cold stress when water temperatures drop below 68°F.*

BELOW: *Manatees are a photographer's dream subject, because they are friendly and cooperative, and spontaneously pose in one appealing position after another.*

BELOW RIGHT: *Three "mermaids," a calf and two adults, quietly rise to the surface at Crystal River National Wildlife Refuge.*

Mermaid folklore is common in cultures throughout the world. Called sea nymphs, tritons, silkies, and sirens, the part-human creatures supposedly used their hypnotic beauty to lure seamen to the depths of the ocean. Repeated "mermaid" sightings by sea-weary sailors probably had much to do with the naming of the order Sirenia—after Homer's tales of bewitching sirens. Even William Shakespeare called manatees "sea-maids" in *A Midsummer Night's Dream*.

"The connection between sirenians and mermaids has persisted through time," wrote John E. Reynolds in *Manatees and Dugongs*. "Perhaps someone observed a sirenian with seaweed on its head, and mistook the vegetation for hair."

"They do look like mermaids," says Seattle photographer Mike Sedam, "ugly mermaids. The first time I saw them, I couldn't believe it. I had no idea manatees even existed. They are the strangest creatures. There is definitely nothing else in the world that looks like them. They really got stuck with a weird body."

Portuguese explorers perpetuated the stories of mermaids and mermen when they encountered dugongs off the coast of Ceylon (modern-day Sri Lanka). In 1560 they captured seven of the strange animals near Mannar in northern Ceylon and shipped them to India. There, the viceroy's physician did a thorough investigation of the mysterious mammals and found the "creatures comparable with humans in every respect."

Because their heads and upper backs often protrude above the surface when they feed, sirenians have been mistaken for people swimming in the water. In 1905 a captain on a freighter traveling through the Red Sea thought he saw three people bobbing in the water up to their chests. Thinking they might be survivors from a shipwreck, he signaled and approached them, only to discover that they were dugongs when they quickly submerged and swam away.

Historical Descriptions and Exploitation

While the English and Dutch nicknamed manatees "sea cows" due to their bovid eating habits, docile manner, and flavorful flesh, no one really knows how the manatee got its common name. According to author Richard Lydekker, the British called them *manatis* (from the Latin *manus*, meaning "hand")—a reference to the handlike use of their flippers when feeding. The word *manati* used by the Carib Indians to describe these creatures means "woman's breast"; the Portuguese and Spanish adopted the term after they invaded the Carib Islands, but their translation of the word meant "with hands."

Both are accurate observations of the manatee. Positioned in the armpit of each flipper, the female's axillary nipples do look somewhat human, as do the front flippers, which appear like giant webbed hands when viewed at certain angles. The five finger bones or "digits," flattened and enfolded in skin, are clearly visible from the underside of each flipper. Vestigial nails located at their tips hint at the manatee's terrestrial origins.

Fossilized manatee bones have been found in Florida that date back at least 45 mil-

"Unbelievable as it may seem, these gentle but very ugly beasts are said to have spawned the mermaid myth. Mermaids? Only a sailor who had been at sea for many months or who had visited one too many bars in port could possibly see beauty in these beasts."

—GEORGE KENSINGER, *in* Strangest Creatures of the World

"Distance must lend enchantment to the view, for it would be a very impressionable and imaginative sailor who, even after many weeks at sea without the company of women, could be allured by the charms of a bristly-muzzled dugong, or mistake the snorting of a wallowing manatee for the love song of a mermaid."

—HENRY LEE, *in* Mermaids and Mastodons, *by R. Carrington, 1957*

RIGHT: *A Florida manatee at Crystal River National Wildlife Refuge shows a hint of "mermaid" as it prepares to take a breath at the surface. With their oval shape and graceful curves, manatees are pleasing to the eye, both as an art form and as an appealing logo for conservation.*

"The resemblance was sufficient for the sea cows to be given the group name Sirenia, after the fabled Sirens of Greek mythology. They were sea nymphs, half women, half birds, who lured love-struck sailors to shipwreck on the rocks by singing to them. Today the story may be given a reverse twist, for the real-life sea cows are slowly but surely being killed off by man."

—ROBERT M. MCCLUNG, *in* Hunted Mammals of the Sea

lion years. In fact, the bones of manatees and dugongs are common in the Pleistocene deposits of the southeastern United States. The Taino Indians of the Greater Antilles in the Caribbean reportedly carved manatee bones into long spoons. Middens (trash heaps) dating from A.D. 400 to 700 on Moko Cay near Belize City have yielded the largest number of manatee bones of any site excavated so far in the Caribbean. The Maya in Mexico used the animals' skins to cover their shields and canoes; in South America, foot coverings made from manatee leather were worn.

Ceremonial smoking pipes in the shape of manatees were used by pre-Columbian Indian tribes in Florida, and manatee bones have been found in their middens. In southern Florida, the animals appear to have had some ritualistic significance, as manatee head bones have been found buried in the graves of tribal chiefs there.

Manatees were increasingly killed in the 1500s for their tender, veal-like meat. In northeastern South America, Guiana Indians used the moku-moku flower suspended above the water surface to bait manatees. When the unsuspecting prey stretched its head out of the water to reach the vegetarian morsels, it was shot with arrows. Miskito Indians in Nicaragua and the Maya in Mexico captured manatees by spearing them with a harpoon attached to a rope that was tied to a floating buoy. Once the animals were tethered, the Miskito clubbed them to death; the Maya simply dragged them to shore and let them die on their own. Indians in Cuba reportedly used tethered remoras (suckerfish) to find and secure manatees.

Upon arriving in the New World, Europeans learned to hunt manatees for their meat, skin, and oil. Buccaneers killed manatees in the Republic of Panama to provision their boats, and Spanish colonists in Central America and Cuba developed a crossbow technique to kill the animals. Manatees, it turned out, were easy to kill. Like oversize puppy dogs, the docile, inquisitive creatures often swam right up to their human captors.

Soon after Columbus explored the Caribbean, the Spanish Catholic church declared manatees a fish so that their meat could be eaten on Fridays. Ironically, in

ABOVE: *The unmistakable silhouette of a manatee is back-lit by morning sunlight as it floats near the surface in the Crystal River.*

ABOVE LEFT: *A mother and calf swim off into the distance, propelled by the graceful up-and-down sweeps of their broad flattened tails.*

1966, the same year that the Endangered Species Preservation Act was first passed in the United States, Pope Paul VI declared that it was no longer a mortal sin to eat meat on Fridays. More than 30 years later, in 1998, the nation's Roman Catholics have once again been urged to return to meatless Fridays—as penance for allowing a "culture of death" (violence and abortions) to take root in the United States.

In Florida, the Timucuan and Seminole Indians harpooned the aquatic mammals they called "big beavers" from canoes and sold excess manatee meat to the Spaniards. The Tekesta Indians of southern Florida also hunted manatees, as described by early Spanish writer Lopez de Velasco:

"When [a hunter] discovers a sea cow he throws his rope around its neck, and as the animal sinks under the water, the Indian drives a stake through one of its nostrils, and no matter how much it may dive, the Indian never loses it, because he goes upon its back."

The Spanish believed that the manatee's inner ear bones held special curative powers. They burned and pulverized the bones (called stones) into a powder and then took a small amount of the powder on a empty stomach in the morning with a swig of white wine. The magic "manatee stones" were supposed to cure just about everything from side aches, colic, and dysentery to kidney problems. In Central and South America, manatee bones are still worn as charms for good luck, to reduce the pain of childbirth, and to bring rain.

Besides tasting like veal or pork, manatee meat had other qualities extolled by early writers. When boiled or fried in its own oil, the meat could apparently be preserved for a year or more. Because of this, an enterprising Dutch company chartered ships in 1643 and sailed to Guyana to capture manatees. The meat was then preserved and shipped to the Caribbean islands, where it was sold as food for slaves.

Rifles made it even easier to slaughter sea cows, and great numbers were killed in the 1700s. European settlers killed manatees for their meat, fat, and hides. Just about every part of the animal was used. The thick skin was cured and crafted into quality leather goods, including walking sticks, horse whips, shoes, and the heavy leather whips once used on slave plantations. Lacking marrow, the dense rib bones were used as weapons and as ivory for ornamental carvings. Even the manatee's body fat and clear oil were used—for lubrication, for food, and as lantern fuel to generate light.

In the late 1800s, a new twist to the manatee slaughter began with the burgeoning era of museums and aquariums. They all wanted manatees for their collections—dead ones. Museums paid $100 for a cleaned manatee skeleton and hide—if there were no detectable harpoon or bullet holes. In the name of science, hunters readily traded in their rifles and spears for seine nets to capture the animals.

Around the same time, another novel idea for exploiting manatees took shape. According to author Tim Dietz, manatees and dugongs are the only known mammals able to convert aquatic plants into protein. Because of this, the concept of raising them like commercial beef cattle for their meat, hide, and bones was proposed several dif-

BELOW: *A Crystal River manatee munches on hydrilla, an exotic plant introduced to Florida in the 1950s. Herbicides sprayed on such aquatic weeds are an indirect threat to manatees.*

ferent times. In 1893 a group of businessmen discussed the possibility of turning 100,000 acres of water south of Miami into a manatee farm, and in 1917 even Alexander Graham Bell discussed the merits of raising manatees commercially. Nothing ever happened, but the name of one small cove in the Florida Keys—Cowpens Key—suggests that at one time manatees may have been held captive there.

Driving such discussions was the popularity of "sea beef" (manatee meat), which was served at many exclusive restaurants at the turn of the century. The tail, especially, was considered a delicacy, eaten cold after being soaked in brine.

"The tail, which forms the most valuable part of the manati, after laying some days in a pickle prepared for it with spices, etc. and eaten cold, is a discovery of which Apicus [Apicius] might have been proud, and which the discriminating palate of Eloyabalus [Elagabalus] would have thought justly entitled to the most distinguished reward," wrote a traveler to the Honduran coast in the 1800s. In less poetic terms, Jamaican poachers still claim that manatee meat tastes remarkably like veal, beef, or pork, depending on which part of the body is eaten.

Utilitarian Uses

The water hyacinth *(Eichhornia crassipes),* native to South America, was introduced into Florida in the 1880s by a Jacksonville woman—because she liked the plant's purple flowers. By the 1960s, the alien species had run amok in Florida's high-nutrient, over-fertilized waters, covering 125,000 acres of public lakes and rivers. While this has turned into an expensive weed-control problem for the state, the prolific plant has been a boon to the manatees, which quickly incorporated it into their herbivorous diet.

Meanwhile, the pesky plant has invaded and clogged Florida's many freshwater habitats, and it routinely threatens boat traffic when it grows into huge floating islands. Blown by the wind, the plants sail across the water surface and pile up into impenetrable heaps, blocking access to docks, boats, and shorelines one day and then disappearing the next. And furthermore, if left unchecked, the exotic water hyacinth disrupts native food chains and fish populations by depleting available oxygen and shading out bottom-dwelling plants. Canadian scientist David Spurgeon of the International Development Research Centre in Ottawa calculated that an acre of the plants imposes an oxygen-depleting load on the water equivalent to the sewage produced by 40 people. Because the plant is so troublesome, and so expensive to control, possession of water hyacinth can lead to a $500 fine and 60 days in jail.

In 1967 biologist James O'Hara estimated that a square meter of pond contained up to 84,000 invertebrate animals if water hyacinths were present. From the tips of the fibrous hanging root masses to the thick canopy of floating leaves, an extraordinary association of creatures inhabit the water-hyacinth rafts: six species of snakes, two eel-like salamanders, turtles, tree frogs, anoles, crustaceans, snails, and aquatic insects, including the alligator flea.

"Singly, the inflorescence of the water hyacinth is a thing of beauty, a spathe of incredibly fragile flowers of an ethereal lavender. But the full impact of hyacinth bloom comes when you see it spread over ten or a hundred acres, or down both sides of a long reach of a river."

꩜

—ARCHIE CARR,
in A Naturalist
in Florida

But as biologically wondrous as this floating canopy might be, possibly supplying manatees with a bit more animal protein than scientists realize, the plants are a big problem. In Guyana, West Indian manatees had been used successfully to clear weed-choked waterways, so it was proposed that Florida's manatees be enlisted to do the same.

According to author Mary Unterbrink, scientists, knowing of the manatee's special taste for water hyacinths, placed two dozen manatees in South Florida canals in the mid-1960s. The canals had become clogged with fast-growing plants, making them impassable and restricting their drainage. The manatees cooperated by eating their favorite treat, but unfortunately, the experiment did not end well. Some of the manatees became sick from algae in the water, others were abused by humans, and a sudden winter freeze caused several more to catch pneumonia and die. The experiment was stopped in 1969 when the few remaining survivors were released into open water.

In 1972 the state introduced two hyacinth-eating weevils (*Neochetina bruchi* and *N. eichhorniae*) into Florida's biota, and in 1977 a hyacinth-eating moth (*Sameodes albiguttalis*) was added to battle the plants. The state also tried using massive doses of herbicidal spray on the plants. The copper-based herbicides used to control the plants, however, subsequently boosted copper levels in manatee tissues. The highest copper levels (1,200 parts per million dry weight) exceeded all previously reported concentrations in livers of wild mammals.

Florida now spends millions of dollars annually to control water hyacinth growing throughout the state, including areas within Everglades National Park. Less toxic her-

ABOVE: *A Crystal River manatee everts its perioral bristles while feeding on hydrilla, an exotic plant native to Sri Lanka.*

bicidal sprays are being used, and in some places the plants are physically corralled with airboats, pulled out on draglines, and then hauled away in dump trucks. All this effort and expense to control the plant with the "pretty purple flower."

Similarly, the state does battle with hydrilla *(Hydrilla verticillata),* an aquatic plant introduced from Sri Lanka in the 1950s as vegetation for aquariums. More than 40 percent of Florida's rivers and lakes are now infested with this exotic, which spreads easily attached to boat propellers and trailers and can produce millions of underground tubers that lie dormant for years. Between 1980 and 1989, Florida spent $48 million trying to control this obnoxious plant.

Yet the ironic twist to this environmental tale of alien aquatic plants is this: As the manatees' native seagrass beds are being destroyed (80 percent have been lost since 1960) by increasing water pollution, boat traffic, and coastal development, exotic species such as water hyacinth and hydrilla have provided the endangered herbivores with an abundant, substitute food supply.

Manatees as Living Art

The peaceful, three-dimensional world of the manatee remained largely obscure until the 1960s, when nature photographers donned wet suits to provide the first underwater views of this unusual marine mammal. The geographic location and generally tur-bid habitat of the West African and Amazonian manatees makes such photography dif-ficult, as is photography of the greatly dispersed Antillean subspecies of the West Indian manatee. Florida manatees, on the other hand, inhabit the northernmost limit of their species' otherwise tropical range. This is possible due to the warm-water refuges, natural and man-made, that are located around peninsular Florida. The warmth-seeking mammals congregate in great numbers at these sites each year to escape the winter-chilled waters, providing ideal, even unique, conditions for underwa-ter photography of these shy, gentle animals. In fact, the clear, spring-fed water of Crystal River is the best, if not only, place that people can legally snorkel and scuba dive with wintering manatees.

The result has been a scientific as well as an artistic body of work that documents not only the natural history of the manatee, but the animal's fascinating underwater beauty. Suspended in a liquid medium, the manatees' graceful movements, curved and rounded bodies, and spoon-shaped tails become an art form unto themselves. Their elliptical bodies seem to transform into a myriad of shapes as they move through the water. In silhouette their oval outlines can be most dramatic. Add the effect of surface sunbursts and mesmerizing shadow ripples played across their skin, and manatees become graphic art. Viewed as such, the three-dimensional curves and planes achieved by these bewhiskered mammals can be quite intriguing, if not pleasing to the eye.

BELOW: *Surface sunlight dances across the mobile canvas of a Crystal River manatee.*

Ancient Marine Herbivores

ACCORDING TO MARINE MAMMALOGIST JOHN E. REYNOLDS, chairman of the U.S. Marine Mammal Commission based in Bethesda, Maryland, the mammals most completely adapted to an aquatic environment belong to two orders: the Cetacea (whales, dolphins, and porpoises) and the Sirenia (manatees and dugongs). These are the only mammals that spend their entire lives in water. However, that's about as far as the similarities go—because the Sirenia share no evolutionary relationship with any major group of living marine mammals.

In fact, the order Sirenia is an interesting offshoot on the evolutionary tree. Classified in the superorder Subungulata, dugongs and manatees evolved from a group of primitive terrestrial ungulates millions of years ago. Over time, their forelimbs flattened into modified flippers (two species still have rudimentary nails), and their hind limbs degenerated, leaving but a vestigial trace of a pelvic girdle that no longer attaches

PRECEDING PAGE: Introduced to Florida in the 1880s, the water hyacinth quickly became a pest species by spreading throughout the state's freshwater habitats. Left uncontrolled, the plant grows into huge floating islands that clog waterways and disrupt boat traffic. Manatees, which eat 10 to 15 percent of their body weight in food each day, help to curb the growth of the plants by acting as aquatic lawn mowers.

BELOW: *Millions of years ago, the manatees' hindlegs degenerated and their tails flattened and enlarged as they took to the sea. Traces of their long-lost hindlimbs can still be seen on their remnant pelvic bones.*

to the backbone. With torpedo-like bodies hydrodynamically streamlined for swimming, the sirenians took to the sea, propelled by their powerful tails. In fact, fossil evidence and blood-protein analysis relate the sirenians not to pinnipeds (seals, sea lions, and walruses) or cetaceans, but to elephants, hyraxes, and aardvarks, whose ancestral line they left onshore millions of years ago.

Living Fossils

According to Richard Barnes of the Karisoke Research Centre in Rwanda, the earliest ungulates, the Condylarthra, appeared in the early Paleocene Epoch about 65 million years ago. They were the ancestors of the modern ungulates, the Perissodactyla (odd-toed ungulates) and the Artiodactyla (even-toed ungulates). The Tubulidentata (aardvarks) diverged from the Condylarthra early on during the Paleocene and specialized in feeding on termites and ants. Another Paleocene offshoot from the Condylarthra gave rise to the Paenungulata (the primitive ungulates or subungulates) in Africa. By the early Eocene, about 54 million years ago, the Paenungulata had separated into three distinct orders, the Hyracoidea (hyraxes), Sirenia (dugongs and manatees), and Proboscidea (elephants).

All three orders are very different in appearance, but they share several features. These include digits with short flattened nails, the absence of clavicle bones and front teeth, similar anatomy of both placenta and womb, two teats between the forelegs (except in the hyraxes), and testes that remain in the body cavity close to the kidneys.

"For several years I have been working with personnel of the Reserve Geologique de Haute Provence at a fossil locality in southeastern France known as Taulanne," says Howard University paleontologist Daryl Domning. "This site, perched in a picturesque mountain valley in the Maritime Alps just inland from the French Riviera, preserves the most abundant remains of Late Eocene sirenians of any place known, and in terms of the number of sirenian bones per cubic meter of sediment it is probably the richest fossil sirenian locality in the world. Indeed, sirenians are almost the only fossil vertebrates found in these rocks."

Given legal protection by the French as a Geological Reserve, the Taulanne site has been developed into a permanent outdoor exhibit showing many of the sirenian bones preserved in situ. A single exposed layer of rock tens of yards long and several yards wide, protected under a thick Plexiglas cover, has been excavated to show scores of sirenian bones chiseled out of the hard limestone. According to Domning, the exhibit gives visitors a snapshot view of the ancient seafloor—at one moment in time.

In the nearby tourist town of Castellane, a new sirenian museum opened next door to city hall in 1998. Decorated on the outside with an impressionistic frieze of mermaids alternating with swimming dugongs, the museum chronicles the geology and paleontology of the Taulanne site. It also traces the evolution of the Sirenia, explains their fascinating biology, and offers a colorful history of mermaid myths and legends.

The fossil record reveals that the Sirenia were once far more diverse and wide-

spread than they are today. At least twenty different genera have been identified in the fossil record. Even though the extinct species differ somewhat in appearance from the modern species, all appear to have been completely aquatic.

The fossil record also shows that both manatees and dugongs once inhabited the New World. Although scientists believe that the Sirenia probably originated in Africa, some of the oldest known fossils have been found in Jamaica. Sirenian fossils 45 million years old have also been found in Florida, along with fossil dugong ribs preserved in the state's many marine sedimentary deposits.

Domning believes that the absence of dugongs in the New World today can be explained by looking at their teeth. He points to the more wear-resistant teeth found in manatees, which enable them to exploit aquatic plants throughout the water column, even along shorelines. In contrast, dugong teeth and snouts are designed to grub whole plants from the bottom. These differences, says Domning, may have given manatees the competitive edge in the New World when it came to exploiting developing areas of freshwater vegetation.

Today only four sirenian species survive. They include the dugong *(Dugong dugon),* restricted to the coastal waters of the Indian and Pacific Oceans, and three species of manatees: the West African manatee *(Trichechus senegalensis),* the Amazonian manatee *(T. inunguis),* and the West Indian manatee *(T. manatus).* Based on anatomical features and current distribution, the West Indian manatee has been further divided into two sub-

LEFT: *Like elephants, manatee calves have a prolonged juvenile dependency. Their very survival depends on the close physical and social bonds they develop with their mothers.*

species, the Florida manatee *(T. m. latirostris)* and the Antillean manatee *(T. m. manatus).* Only the West African manatee is listed as a threatened species under the U.S. Endangered Species Act—the other three sirenian species are listed as endangered.

According to Reynolds, all four species are united by the following traits: large spindle-shaped or fusiform bodies; absence of external hind limbs; pectoral flippers; large flattened tails; heavy bones that are thick and swollen (pachyostotic) and very hard and solid (osteosclerotic); relatively small brains in comparison to body size; lack of an

RIGHT: *The similarities between manatees and elephants are many. They reveal their common ancestry in their teeth, flattened toenails, prehensile upper lips, large digestive tract, herbivorous diet, and location of the mammary glands. Here a manatee calf nurses from a teat located beneath the mother's flipper.*

externally distinct neck; specialized teeth; very sparse body hair; and the presence of horny plates in the mouth that are used to help crush ingested plant material.

The sirenians reached their peak in abundance and diversity millions of years ago. Nobody knows why they declined. The four species that remain are relict species, survivors from a once more pervasive order of aquatic, plant-eating mammals. As such, dugongs and manatees are vital biological links with the long evolutionary history of life on this planet. They are living fossils that preserve a genetic code from a time and age long past.

ABOVE: *A manatee skull shows many of the physical traits shared with elephants: a massive lower jaw, no front teeth, and grinding molars in the back of the mouth that migrate forward as they wear out.*

Elephant Cousins

A more unlikely family tree can hardly be imagined for marine mammals that are helpless on land yet perfectly adapted for life in a liquid environment. Yet studies using biochemical analysis of proteins show that the terrestrial Proboscidea (elephants) and Hyracoidea (hyraxes), and the more distant Tubulidentata (aardvarks), are the closest modern relatives to manatees and dugongs. Although elephants and hyraxes are now separated from the sirenians in evolutionary time and space, not to mention physical appearance, the sirenians still share many common traits recognizable in their distant terrestrial relatives.

For example, both elephants and sirenians are long-lived herbivores that can survive 50 to 60 years or more. They have large bodies in comparison to brain size, slow metabolic rates, and extensive digestive tracts needed to accommodate a diet of bulky plant food. Both have short necks, dense bones, regenerating molars, testes that remain within the body cavity, and a pair of mammary glands located between the front limbs. Highly

LEFT: *An African elephant curls its prehensile trunk and shows off its large tusks (upper canine teeth) in Kenya's Amboseli National Park. Elephants, hyraxes, and aardvarks evolved from the same primitive ungulates millions of years ago—as did the Sirenia. (Photo by Windland Rice/Jeff Foott Productions)*

sensitive to touch, elephants and sirenians have prehensile upper lips and sensitive skin covered with sparse tactile hairs. These social animals use touch and vocalizations to communicate with one another, particularly between mother and calf during the calf's prolonged period of juvenile dependency. West Indian and West African manatees even have flat, elephant-like toenails located at the ends of their flippers.

Probably the most formidable similarity between elephants and sirenians is that of extinction. At one time, many different species of elephants inhabited the earth. Today only two genera remain, with one species each: the African elephant *(Loxodonta africana)* and the Asian elephant *(Elephas maximus)*. They are part of the group of animals, including the hyraxes, sirenians, and aardvarks, that evolved from primitive ungulates in Lower Tertiary Africa.

Hyrax Relatives

Most people are surprised to learn that the marmotlike animal called a hyrax is not a rodent at all but a member of its own separate order, the Hyracoidea. As such, hyraxes are classified as primitive ungulates within the same superorder (Paenungulata) as elephants and sirenians.

The hyrax's identity has been almost as confused as that of the sirenians. At first hyraxes were mistakenly linked with guinea pigs of the genus *Cavia,* which is why their family name is Procaviidae, or "before the guinea pigs." After this mistake was discovered, the small furry mammals were given the name "hyrax," which means "shrew mouse." Not until the 19th century did zoologists realize that hyraxes are taxonomically related to pachyderms, not rodents. Like elephants and sirenians, hyraxes are subungulates—the last survivors of a large group of primitive plant-eating animals that evolved in Africa.

In Hebrew and Phoenician, hyraxes are called *shaphan,* which means "the hidden one." There are eleven different species in three genera. Weighing 3 to 10 pounds, hyraxes live in tree, bush, and rock habitats. Their feet have four toes in front and three in back, and they lack an externally visible tail. Long tactile hairs (also present on manatee skin) protrude at intervals all over their bodies and probably help them orient in dark fissures and holes. Rock hyraxes have protruding upper incisors that appear to reflect their phylogenetic relationship to elephants. In fact, several African tribes called hyraxes the "little brothers of elephants" long before taxonomists reached the same evolutionary conclusion.

Forty-million-year-old fossils discovered in Egypt show that hyraxes were once widespread, medium-size grazing and browsing ungulates. At one time, six genera existed. Competition from the even-toed ungulates reduced hyrax populations to tree and rock habitats roughly 25 million years ago. Yet the animals remained widespread, radiating from southern Europe into China. Today these unusual mammals can be found only in Africa and the Middle East.

Hyraxes retain several primitive features. They have a low metabolic rate and a poor ability to regulate body temperature. In addition to primitive short feet, they also

ABOVE: *Hyraxes, native to Africa and the Middle East, have retained several primitive features shared with elephants, manatees, and dugongs: they have a low metabolic rate, poor ability to regulate body temperature, and they use their molars to crop food rather than their incisors as most modern hoofed mammals do. (Photo by Windland Smith/Jeff Foott Productions)*

have an inefficient feeding mechanism. To crop food, they use their molars rather than their incisors, as modern hoofed mammals do.

According to German biologist Hendrik Hoeck, hyraxes maintain their body temperature through gregarious huddling, by basking in sunlight, and through relatively short bursts of activity offset by long periods of inactivity. They are able to digest fiber efficiently by means of microbial digestion. Their specialized physiology allows them to exist on food of poor quality in very dry areas—but only in environments where temperature and humidity remain relatively constant.

BELOW: *Although it may seem surprising, this manatee's relatives include the elephant, the hyrax, and even the aardvark.*

Where Sirenians Live

THE SIRENIA ARE THE ONLY PRIMARILY PLANT-EATING marine mammals alive today. Of the nearly two dozen genera identified through the fossil record, only two have survived into the 20th century. One is represented by the dugong *(Dugong dugon),* a species inhabiting the coastal waters of the Indo-Pacific. The other comprises three species of manatees in the family Trichechidae: the Amazonian manatee *(Trichechus inunguis),* found in the Amazon River basin of South America; the West African manatee *(T. senegalensis)* of tropical West Africa; and the West Indian manatee *(T. manatus),* found from the southeastern United States throughout the Caribbean and eastern Central America to the northeastern coast of South America.

A fifth species of sirenian, the Steller's sea cow *(Hydrodamalis gigas),* existed as recently as 1768, when the last animal was killed by an infamous hunter named Ivan Popov. Steller's sea cow is still included in descriptions of the Sirenia because of the

PRECEDING PAGE: *In parts of the world, manatees are viewed with superstition. One South American tribe believes that manatees are bewitched human beings that live in cities at the bottom of rivers.*

"According to native folklore in Mexico, the male manatee sometimes comes ashore on dark nights and carries off the women in the villages along river banks."

∾

—GEORGE GOODWIN, *in* The Animal Kingdom, *1954*

LEFT: *A Crystal River manatee glides by, showing its hydro-dynamically designed shape. From blood type to reproduction, manatees remain so similar to pachyderms that they could be called "sea elephants."*

species' recent demise. Most important, it is the only sirenian genus across a 45-million-year-old fossil record that succumbed to human hunters.

Steller's Sea Cow

Just 230 years ago, the magnificent Steller's sea cow *(Hydrodamalis gigas)* took its last breath into extinction. Also known as the Great Northern sea cow, this huge plant-eating mammal was discovered in the Bering Sea in 1741. Unlike the other more tropical-dwelling sirenian species, this gigantic herbivore lived in cold subarctic waters. Lacking finger bones in their tiny flippers—and functional teeth—Steller's sea cows fed almost exclusively on marine algae (kelp).

With disproportionately small heads and bilobed tails, these harmless, rotund marine mammals weighed between 4 and 10 metric tons and stretched 26 feet or more in length. As protection against the elements, they were covered with thick, brown, bark-like skin, sometimes streaked with white. Apparently unable to dive because of their great buoyancy, the sea cows grazed head down with their backs exposed above the surface in the offshore kelp beds around Bering and Copper Islands. Lacking teeth, they used horny grinding plates located in the front of their mouths to crush their plant food.

As part of a Russian exploratory expedition, German naturalist Georg Wilhelm Steller discovered the sea cows while shipwrecked on Bering Island in 1741. By reviewing subsequent log books and harvest records, naturalist Leonard Stejneger estimated that there must have been about 2,000 sea cows at the time. In 1755, after seeing that they had disappeared from Copper Island, a Russian mining engineer named Jakovleff filed a formal petition asking authorities to stop the wasteful harvest of these animals. His petition was ignored, and in 1768, just 13 years later, and a mere 27 years after they were first discovered, the huge docile sea cows were extinct—hunted into oblivion by a hungry bipedal omnivore named *Homo sapiens.*

Fortunately, Steller made detailed records of the sea cow's habits for the 10 months of his shipwrecked stay on Bering Island. He described sea cow herds gathering at the mouths of freshwater brooks located around the island and their coming so close to shore during flood tides that one could touch them. He observed protective adults shield their calves from intruders and rocky shorelines, and he witnessed sea cows smothered by ice in winter and dashed against cliffs in storm surges. And he watched the rotund sea cows rest in quiet coves, where they would float belly up, lulled on the ocean swells. Most poignant of all, Steller described how members of a herd would try to help an injured or tethered animal escape from its human captors, often returning for several days to the site where an animal had been dragged onto the shore and butchered.

"To this end," wrote Steller, "some of them tried to upset the boat with their backs, while others pressed down the rope and endeavored to break it, or strove to remove the hook from the wound in the back by blows of their tail, in which they actually succeeded several times. It is a most remarkable proof of their conjugal affection that the male, after having tried with all his might, although in vain, to free the female caught

"These mighty sirenians of the north differed from their tropical relatives in size and in the nature of their skin. The skin is black, irregular, wrinkled, coarse, lacks hairs, and is penetrated by vertical tubules. The skin looks more like an oak tree's bark than the skin of an animal."

∽

—BERNARD GRZIMEK,
in Animal Life
Encyclopedia

SIRENIANS OF THE WORLD
ORDER: SIRENIA (Sea Cows)

West African Manatee *length 10-13'*

WEST INDIAN MANATEE

length 10-13'

Amazonian Manatee *length 10'*

Dugong *length 8'-13'*

Steller's Sea Cow *length 24'-30' (EXTINCT)*

Subspecies:
Trichechus manatus latirostris (Florida manatee)
Trichechus manatus manatus (Antillean manatee)

by the hook, and in spite of the beating we gave him, nevertheless followed her to shore, and that several times, even after she was dead, he shot unexpectedly up to her like a speeding arrow."

Steller described the sea cow's blubber as being 3 to 4 inches thick: "Melted, it tastes so sweet and delicious that we lost all desire for butter. In taste it comes pretty close to the oil of sweet almonds." One animal supplied the entire camp with meat, said to be indistinguishable from beef, for up to two weeks, during which time the meat stayed edible, even during the hottest summer days. Hunters ate the meat and used the tough skin to make boat covers and shoe leather.

With the passing of Steller's sea cow in 1768, lost to science was an extraordinary marine mammal that was unlike any in existence—or that will ever live again. Only two marine mammals have gone extinct in modern times—the Caribbean monk seal *(Monachus tropicalis)* and Steller's sea cow. Because no complete skeleton from a Steller's sea cow was ever found, the ten *Hydrodamalis* skeletons that still exist are all composites, made from the parts of several animals. One of these can be viewed at Harvard University, where it hangs in unceremonious oblivion in a remote corner of the Museum of Comparative Zoology.

ABOVE: *Pictured in this Sirenia poster are the dugong, three living species of manatees, and the extinct Steller's sea cow. (Reproduced with permission of Save the Manatee Club and the Florida Department of Environmental Protection)*

ABOVE: *Unlike manatees, dugongs have fluked, or whale-like, tails. (Photo © Doug Perrine/Innerspace Visions)*

ABOVE RIGHT: *Found throughout the warm coastal waters of the Indo-Pacific, dugongs are the most marine and most widely distributed of all sirenian species. This mother and calf were photographed off the coast of Australia. (Photo © Saul Gonor/Innerspace Visions)*

RIGHT: *In this photograph, taken in the Indonesian waters, it is easy to see the distinctive horseshoe-shaped muzzle of a dugong. (Photo © David B. Fleetham/Innerspace Visions)*

The Dugong

The dugong *(Dugong dugon)* is the closest living relative of Steller's sea cow. A widely distributed species that inhabits the tropical and subtropical coastal waters of the Indian and Pacific Oceans, dugongs are found in the greatest numbers in the seagrass meadows of northern Australia and Papua New Guinea, as well as along the shores of 43 different countries. The most marine of all the sirenian species, they are listed as Vulnerable by the International Union for the Conservation of Nature and Natural Resources, now simply called the IUCN–World Conservation Union, in their Red List of Threatened Animals, and "endangered" under the U.S. Endangered Species Act.

The name "dugong" is derived from the Malayan word *duyong,* but this is just one of the animal's many international names. In Arabic-speaking countries it is called *arus-al-bahr,* meaning "mermaid" or "bride of the sea." In Madagascar its name is *lambon-dana,* or "wild pig of the coral." Natives on the Nicobar Islands call it *suar machhi,* or "pigfish," and in Mozambique it is known as *n'pfuwomati,* or the "sea hippo." In Sri Lanka it is simply called *kandal pandi*—the "sea pig."

Unlike manatees, the slightly smaller dugongs have split tail flukes, a few permanent molars, and down-turned muzzles designed for bottom feeding, and their skin is smoother. The end of the muzzle flattens out into a horseshoe-shaped facial or rostral disk that enables them to pull whole plants from the seafloor. Another big difference is that male dugongs grow two short tusks (modified upper incisor teeth), which erupt when they are about 12 to 15 years old. The tusks protrude through the upper lip and are thought to aid in courtship. Unlike manatees, dugong males appear to fight for access to estrous females, using splashing, tail thrashing, body rolls, and lunges in an attempt to compete for an opportunity to mate.

Whether they are highly gregarious or simply attracted to prime feeding areas, large groups of dugongs with 100 or more animals have been observed off the Australian coast and in the Arabian Gulf. In the early 19th century, an enormous herd was recorded off Brisbane, Australia, that reportedly covered an area 3.5 by 1.5 miles across. Dugongs share their seagrass pastures with herbivorous sea turtles and several large, meat-eating predators—saltwater crocodiles, sharks, and killer whales.

Dugongs have never been bred in captivity. All available information about their reproductive behavior has been obtained by studying their carcasses. According to biologist Helene Marsh at Queensland's James Cook University, dugongs are even slower breeders than manatees. Both sexes take 9 to 10 years to reach sexual maturity, and some females don't even reproduce until they are 15 to 17 years of age. With a gestation period that lasts about 13 months and calves that continue to nurse for a year and a half or longer (even though they start eating seagrass soon after birth), Marsh estimates that dugongs produce a calf every 3 to 7 years—once they begin breeding.

Such a slow reproductive rate would be ideal for a long-lived animal like the dugong, which can live 70 years or more—if not for humans. Because an adult dugong can yield 200 to 300 pounds of meat, and 18 to 34 quarts of oil, they have been hunted

"Its face is as ugly as its name is beautiful, if one can call it a face at all. Its mouth —or rather its snout—is incredibly wide, has cleft lips and veritable tusks. The bulging eyes protrude from the sockets, the nose looks as though it had been squashed. . . . From the waist down the creature is a fish with a forked tail."

ༀ

—TRANSLATED BY FRENCH PRIEST PÈRE LABAT IN 1732 *from a book on Africa written by an Italian named Cavazzi*

throughout history. The Torres Strait islanders, who live in a dugong-rich area between Australia and New Guinea, have a long cultural tradition of hunting dugongs, whose ribs and skulls decorate their huts. This is reflected in their language: it contains 27 terms to distinguish the age, size, sex, social groupings, color, and taste qualities of dugongs—and 45 more names for the different cuts of meat produced during the butchering process. Unfortunately—from a breeding standpoint—the islanders prefer the meat and fat from an *ipika dangal,* an adult female dugong.

According to Randall Reeves in *Seals and Sirenians,* dugongs have been pursued by human hunters throughout their range. They have been caught in tidal traps and special nets, speared, and killed using sticks of dynamite. Off the coast of Papua New Guinea, they are harpooned and roped by native hunters and upended in the water until they drown. Dugong hides are used to make leather goods, their bones and tusks are used for carvings, and their teeth are worn on necklaces.

Some indigenous cultures believe dugong oil has special medicinal and cosmetic properties. In the Philippines, powdered dugong bone is used as an aphrodisiac. In the Aru Islands of Indonesia, fishermen use dugong tusks as cigarette holders and sell dugong "tears" as an aphrodisiac. According to John E. Reynolds in his book *Manatees and Dugongs,* a cotton swab used to dab dugong tears costs about $1 and is supposed to bring "good luck, prosperity, and success with women."

Worldwide, dugong populations are declining as the result of hunting, habitat destruction, and drownings in fishnets. There is also some evidence that indicates dugongs are susceptible to capture stress. This means that even if a dugong manages to escape from a hunter, or a mesh net, it may later die from the stress of having been pursued and temporarily captured.

Until recently, the waters of northern Australia, including the Great Barrier Reef Marine Park, offered dugongs the greatest protection. But since 1986, dugongs have shown a rapid and catastrophic (50 percent) decline in numbers along a 1,250-mile stretch of the Queensland coast. In 1992 alone, 380 square miles of seagrass habitat were lost. In the meantime, mesh fishnets continue to drown dugongs as seagrass beds disappear in the wake of rapid development—and the military has detonated underwater explosives in the prime dugong habitat of Shoalwater Bay.

The Great Barrier Reef Ministerial Council has endorsed measures for dugong recovery and conservation along the coast, including the establishment of "Dugong Protection Areas" in the animals' key habitats. According to Helene Marsh, the effectiveness of these measures will depend on the political will to exclude mesh netting and to control boating activity and coastal development, along with continued support from indigenous groups to maintain their moratoriums on traditional hunting in this region.

"So far, the indigenous peoples have been by far the most cooperative stakeholder group," says Marsh. "Given that their association with dugongs goes back thousands of years, they understandably consider they have the most to lose by the extinction of dugongs along this coast."

"Even the dugong's so-called tears, which consist of a viscous substance that is secreted from the animal's eyes when it is taken out of water, were valued. The Malays believed that this fluid had powerful influences as an aphrodisiac."

∽

—ROBERT M. McCLUNG, *in* Hunted Mammals of the Sea

Amazonian Manatee

"What animal swims like a dolphin, eats grass like a cow, has flesh that resembles beef, pork, or fish, can replace its worn-out teeth without limit by new ones, and is barely visible in its natural habitat?" asked Daryl Domning, Howard University paleontologist and editor of *Sirenews*. Although this description encompasses all manatees, Domning was referring specifically to the Amazonian manatee *(Trichechus inunguis),* the only species of manatee found in the upper regions of the Amazon and Orinoco Rivers.

Called *peixe-boi* ("ox-fish") in Portuguese and *vaca marina* ("sea cow") in Spanish, the Amazonian manatee inhabits the freshwaters of the vast Amazon Basin. It is the most highly specialized of the three living manatee species, and the smallest—measuring up to 9.2 feet. Not only is it the only species that lives entirely in freshwater, but its skin is smoother than that of the other two species and has distinctive white or pink patches on the underside. Amazonian manatees also have fewer ribs and lack the characteristic "fingernails" on their flippers.

According to Domning, fossils from the upper Amazon Basin suggest that, probably less than five million years ago, the manatees of this region still looked much like modern Florida manatees. However, as they adapted to the peculiar freshwater environment of Amazonia, they underwent many changes—in chromosome number, skeletal structure, and outward appearance. Lost were the vestigial fingernails that hinted of their terrestrial ancestry. Even the complexity of their tooth cusp pattern increased, as did the length of their flippers.

LEFT: *Amazonian manatees inhabit the remote freshwater rivers and tributaries of the Amazon Basin, where habitat destruction, pollution, and illegal hunting have endangered these unique animals. (Photo © Fernando Trujillo/Innerspace Visions)*

Since prehistoric times, the Amazonian manatee has been hunted for its meat, fat, and skin. During the 1930s, it fueled a short-lived Brazilian industry that converted the manatees' thick hides into machinery belts. Even now that the Amazonian manatee is listed as endangered and is legally protected, Brazilian hunters still occasionally kill the animals for food and lantern oil.

Manatees have been known to science since the early 16th century, yet the Amazonian manatee was not recognized as a separate species until 1830. It remained relatively unknown for almost another century and a half, until studies of wild and captive *Trichechus inunguis* were begun in 1975 at the Instituto Nacional de Pesquisas da Amazonia (INPA)—the National Institute of Amazonian Research—located 5 miles from downtown Manaus in the heart of the species' Brazilian Amazon range. Under the direction of American scientist Robin Best, Projecto Peixe-Boi—the Brazilian Manatee Project—produced most of the information available on this species.

Long persecuted by hunters, Amazonian manatees are extremely elusive and difficult to observe in the wild. Murky water makes underwater observation impossible, and huge mats of floating vegetation conceal the mammals when they quietly surface in lakes and rivers to breathe, exposing only the tips of their snouts. This posed a problem for research scientists in need of manatee subjects to observe.

The problem was solved when INPA scientists developed a program to rescue manatee calves orphaned by poachers. Wealthy businesspeople had created a black-market demand for manatee calves as illegal "pet" status symbols. Because of the money involved, hunters killed female manatees to capture their nursing calves. However, lacking adequate food and round-the-clock care, the unweaned orphans invariably died slow deaths from starvation.

Through trial and error, INPA scientists developed a technique for raising orphaned calves on a formula of powdered milk mixed with liquid vitamins and butter. Fed eight to ten times a day through a handheld syringe fitted with a nipple, many of the rescued calves survived to become weaned and well-fed research subjects.

Amazonian manatees live in an exotic environment with prehistoric-looking river fish and jungles teeming with tropical wildlife. They share their Amazonian habitat with pink river dolphins and South American estuarine dolphins, and in the mouth of the Amazon River, their range also overlaps with that of the West Indian manatee. Predation by sharks, caimans, and jaguars has been documented. However, Amazonian manatees are most vulnerable to human hunters when they are forced to congregate in restricted habitats during the dry season.

Amazonian manatees have adapted to an environment with seasonal extremes. In the central Amazon Basin, water levels can vary by 30 to 45 feet. During the summer flood season the manatees disperse widely over floodplain channels and lakes, but as water levels drop in late summer and fall, the manatees move into the deeper pools and channels of large rivers and lakes. During a prolonged dry season in 1979–1980, the late Robin Best observed 500 to 1,000 manatees go for nearly seven months without food, surviving on their fat reserves while confined to a Brazilian lake.

"The Amazon system includes over 200 major tributaries, two of which are over a thousand miles in length, and discharges nearly three billion gallons of water per minute into the Atlantic Ocean. At its mouth, the Amazon is over 200 miles wide and completely surrounds an island the size of France. The Amazon is larger than many seas."

ᘉᖽ

—JAMES R. HOLLAND, *in* The Amazon

Probably the most famous Amazonian manatee known to the American public was a captive animal named Butterball. This baby-faced manatee was a popular resident at San Francisco's Steinhart Aquarium at the California Academy of Sciences from 1967 to 1984—the only captive Amazonian manatee to live in North America. His existence wasn't always so pampered, however. At an early age, Butterball was harpooned by hunters somewhere along the Amazon River and taken to a fish market in Leticia, Colombia. Destined for a stewpot, the baby manatee was saved when a trustee of the academy spotted the little fellow in the market. The stricken calf was purchased and flown to San Francisco, where Steinhart Aquarium veterinarians nursed him back to health. Apparently his wound was so difficult to suture that plastic buttons were used for reinforcement.

Butterball became the subject of numerous scientific studies during the 17 years that he lived at the aquarium and was the focus of several scientific articles, two master's theses, and part of a doctoral dissertation. In addition, the species' karyotype—its characteristic chromosome configuration—was identified from cell samples drawn from Butterball. It turns out that Amazonian manatees have 56 chromosomes, while the West Indian manatees have only 48.

The divers who kept the lonely manatee company described him as "a very wonderful combination of shyness and curiosity." He liked to be rubbed with a thick bristle scrub brush and would swim over and nudge a diver in the legs to receive more scratching. When the divers were in the tank, Butterball vocalized quite a lot with squeaks and chirps.

According to former aquarium director John McCosker, Butterball was the most expensive of all the animals maintained at the Steinhart Aquarium, consuming up to 50 pounds of greenery each day, or more than $6,500 worth of feed each year. To help defray the cost, McCosker solicited academy members for help: "The aquarium wouldn't mind finding a manatee lover to sponsor Butterball—ideally, someone with financial interests in lettuce or red cabbage," he said.

Not all Amazonian manatees had it so good. According to author Randall Reeves, between 1935 and 1954 an estimated 80,000 to 140,000 manatees were killed for their hides, which were used to make machine belts, glue, hoses, high-pressure valves, and cords for cotton looms. An estimated 6,500 manatees were killed in 1959 alone to satisfy a commercial and domestic demand for dried and salted manatee meat and *mixira*—manatee meat preserved in its own fat.

South American fishermen learned to exploit the manatee's strong maternal instinct by capturing the calves first to use as lures to entice the protective females within harpoon range. After harpooning a manatee, the *mariscadores*—subsistence fishermen along the remote tributaries of the Amazon River—often suffocated their winded prey by hammering wooden pegs into their nostrils.

Even though the Amazonian manatee has been protected by law since 1973, enforcement remains a problem because of their remote habitats and distribution across international boundaries. In 1986, following a study of the species in

Ecuador, Robert Timm concluded that habitat destruction, pollution resulting from oil exploration, illegal hunting pressure to supply meat to the military, as well as subsistence to indigenous peoples living along the rivers have made the continued existence of manatees in Ecuador questionable. They are also close to extinction in Colombia and Peru.

West African Manatee

The West African manatee *(Trichechus senegalensis)* inhabits the quiet coastal lagoons, estuaries, interconnected lakes, and large rivers of 20 different African countries. The species' Latin name *(senegalensis)* reflects its northern range in Senegal. From the Senegal River in the north to Angola's Cuanza River in the south, this little-studied species lives in turbid habitats that have made underwater observation difficult, if not impossible, in all but a few locations.

Similar in size, shape, and behavior to the West Indian manatee, the African species has the same wrinkled skin covered with sparse sensory hairs, along with vestigial nails on their flippers. This reflects the fact that the two species share a more similar habitat than with that of the Amazonian manatee. In fact, paleontologists have proposed that the West African species probably arose less than 5 million years ago, when West Indian manatees wandered across the Atlantic.

Since then, the West African species has developed a blunter snout with a less downward-directed rostrum, a less robust body, and noticeably different, more protruding eyes. There are also subtle differences in the cranial bones that separate the two species.

Beginning in the mid-1980s, James "Buddy" Powell was one of the first scientists to study the West African manatee—in parts of Cameroon, Gambia, Mali, Senegal, Nigeria, Guinea Bissau, and Côte d'Ivoire. By radio-tracking individual animals, he found that in many areas these shy, secretive mammals are often most active at night, resting on the bottom by day. Like the West Indian manatee they require calm, warm water (64°F. or above) and access to adequate food and freshwater sources.

At Powell's Côte d'Ivoire study area, the manatees preferred the coastal lagoons. In Nigeria, they moved in and out of oxbows, lakes, and large river pools in the lower Benue River system. In Senegal, they often got trapped by falling water levels in lakes and tributaries that connect to the Senegal River. In Gambia, they ranged along the coast, in estuaries and far up rivers. Powell proposed that the daily and seasonal movements he observed occurred in response to tides and to dry- and wet-season changes in salinity and water levels.

Called *lamantin* by French-speaking Africans (which refers to the female manatee's lamentations upon seeing its calf killed) and *seekuh* or *manati* by the Germans, West African manatees have attracted many fascinating tribal names across their African range. In Gabon they are called *manga*. In Liberia and several other countries they are known as "mammy-water," for a mythical, humanlike river animal that is often regarded with dread and superstition.

"The manatee is one of the most difficult of all mammals to observe. It is shy, secretive, and lives in murky waters."

—ROGER CARAS,
in Vanishing Wildlife

Manatees, it turns out, do not always generate mermaid fantasies, as was discovered by Yale University student Melissa Grigione in the 1980s. In Cameroon, Akwen fishermen told her that manatees are dangerous and that they can drown people. A vice chief from the Egbekaw village agreed that manatees are dangerous and not easily killed, and he warned that it is not worth risking one's life to eat one. A fisherman from the village of Akpasang explained to Grigione that manatees receive power from the devil, and that if a person kills one without first having had traditional training in manatee hunting, the animal would punish the hunter's family.

In 1986 and 1987 in Sierra Leone, Randall Reeves observed hunters waiting on baited platforms to spear hungry manatees enticed with fresh cassava peels and cut grass. They also used fence traps to capture manatees in mangrove areas, dropping a trapdoor behind them once inside and then axing them to death. Chain, twine, and large mesh nets are used to catch them as well. Reeves also observed hunters in the Bonthe and Pujehun districts of Sierra Leone use spear traps. In these, a net, strung across the opening between two posts, serves as a trigger mechanism. When a manatee swims into the net, a spear, sprung with the force of a heavy log behind it, drives deep into the animal; impaled, it either drowns or must wait to be dispatched by a hunter.

The Mende of Sierra Leone view manatees as pests, claiming they tear gill nets, plunder rice fields, and destroy the fish in their nets by sucking the meat right off the bones. Based on the stomach contents of a few West African manatees, it appears that they do occasionally eat clams.

In contrast, the Kalabari people of the Niger delta, reports Reeves, view manatees not as pests, but as sacred animals, even reincarnated human beings. As a result, should someone kill a manatee, they take certain traditional steps to appease the wounded spirit of the dead animal: The hunter remains indoors for three days, rubbing his body with yellow powder and cam wood, while the women of the house sing to the animal's spirit at dawn and dusk.

Elsewhere in Nigeria, where manatees often swim 1,250 miles up the Niger River, Reeves watched villagers living on Lake Kainji capture manatees by using a line rigged with several hundred large hooks. Anchored from shore, the line is strung across the Niger River during the dry season. Suspended just above the river bottom in the turbid water, the hooks snag the passing manatees.

"Although legally protected for several decades in most countries where they regularly occur," says Reeves, "West African manatees are still hunted, trapped, and netted for food over much of their range. Unfortunately, few well-guarded parks or reserves contain substantial numbers of manatees."

According to marine biologist John E. Reynolds, scientists lack adequate knowledge regarding the size of existing West African manatee populations, precisely where they are located, the animals' age-specific reproduction and mortality rates, frequency and causes of mortality, and their social behavior. "Imagine," he says, "trying to conserve and manage a species that occupies a number of separate countries and for which so little information exists."

"We live here on a big round time share, and if we as humans want to assume the role as landlord, then we have to take care of all the tenants."

∽

—JIMMY BUFFETT,
cofounder of Save the Manatee Club

West Indian Manatee

The West Indian manatee *(Trichechus manatus)* is the most widely studied of the four sirenian species. There are two subspecies, the Florida manatee *(T. m. latirostris)* and the Antillean manatee *(T. m. manatus)*. Differences in cranial features and geographic distribution separate the two subspecies. Such a taxonomic subdivision was first proposed in 1934, but not until the 1980s did scientists have enough anatomical evidence to support it.

Historically, this species was found in shallow coastal waters, estuaries, rivers, and lakes of the tropical and subtropical regions along the New World Atlantic coast. The Antillean subspecies ranges throughout the Caribbean islands, from Texas along the east coast of Central America, to the northern coast of South America as far south as Brazil. The Florida subspecies primarily inhabits the coastal waters of peninsular Florida and southern Georgia, ranging as far west as Texas and as far north as Rhode Island. According to Randall Reeves, this suggests that the full range for the species may have extended to the limits of the 24°C. mean annual isotherm in both the Northern and Southern Hemispheres.

Completion of the Panama Canal in 1914 opened up more than shipping routes between the Atlantic and Pacific Oceans—it has allowed faunal traffic to pass through as well. According to Reeves, West Indian manatees entered the Pacific Ocean through the canal in 1984. "Manatees or manatee-like animals have been absent from the eastern Pacific Ocean for several million years," says Reeves. "It will be interesting to see if the dispersal continues and a population becomes established in the Pacific."

In Puerto Rico, the Roosevelt Roads Naval Station provides unofficial sanctuary for a portion of the island's small manatee population. With human activity restricted for security reasons, the manatees safely congregate in the protected coves, feeding on seagrass and drinking freshwater effluents from a nearby sewer plant.

Such manatee havens are all too few, as outside of the United States, the popularity of manatee meat coupled with habitat loss continues to threaten this species. In many parts of the animals' historic range, they are already gone. The manatees have been extirpated from most areas of northern Mexico and are completely absent from a 900-mile stretch of Venezuela's Caribbean coastline. Not only does this represent a major break in the species' historic range, it effectively separates manatee populations in Central America from those on the Atlantic coast of South America.

Surveys indicate that there are only 25 to 30 manatees left in Trinidad and Tobago, and the population is falling. Destruction of mangroves and wetlands for agricultural development is probably the most serious threat to their survival, followed by poaching and pollution. As a result, the West Indian manatee is considered one of the most critically endangered animals in Trinidad and Tobago.

Brazil continued to report commercial catches of manatees in government statistics through the 1980s, at the same time carved and polished manatee ribs were showing up at public markets in the Dominican Republic. Illegal hunting continues in parts of Mexico, Belize, Guatemala, Honduras, and Nicaragua. Off the coast of Belize, plastic gill nets used for fishing sometimes trap, entangle, and drown manatees as the animals patrol the shoreline for food and mates. In Jamaica, such an accidental manatee catch is equivalent to winning the lottery. The animal can fetch $1,000 or more when butchered and sold illegally at market.

Belize is home to the largest remaining population of the Antillean subspecies. However, in and around Port Honduras, hunting manatees has become a quick and easy way to make a living. Even though it is illegal to kill manatees under Belizean and Guatemalan law, the relic custom of eating manatee meat has kept the hunters in business.

"The black market on manatee meat thrives in part," says Will Heyman of The Nature Conservancy, "because the people who buy it are unaware that manatees are an endangered species on the verge of extinction."

"People still think there is an abundance of manatee," adds Wil Maheia of the Belize Center for Environmental Studies. "We need to dispel this myth."

BELOW: *Four West Indian manatees bask in the Crystal River's warm spring water during the cold of winter.*

Natural History of a Plump Sea Nymph

FOR THE FIRST HALF OF THE 20TH CENTURY, THE MANATEE'S aquatic habitat and shy, reclusive behavior hampered long-term studies of its natural history and behavior. Not until 1951, when Joseph Moore published an account of his studies of manatees in the Miami River, did this begin to change. Even so, up until the 1960s, most of what was known about the gentle mammals was gleaned from lab dissection, the study of skeletal remains, and random observations in the wild.

In 1967 Daniel Hartman and his field assistant, James "Buddy" Powell, began an 18-month study of manatee ecology and behavior in Florida's Crystal River. Unlike at other winter aggregation sites used by Florida manatees, food supplies were abundant here due to the proliferation of alien aquatic plants introduced into Florida's waterways. And not only were manatees attracted to Crystal River's warm-water springs, but so were people, who began swimming with them at King's Bay in the 1960s.

"When not resorting to springs for warmth, manatees typically inhabit turbid waters," wrote Hartman *(National Geographic,* September 1969). "This makes observation difficult, and the literature is full of irresponsible anecdotes based on surface glimpses."

On an average winter morning, Hartman would snorkel with his subjects for three to four hours at a time, wearing a second rubber suit over his wet suit for warmth. He spent afternoons tracking their movements, identifying them, and checking social behavior by peering into the water through a glass-bottomed bucket.

From his research, Hartman estimated the basic reproductive traits of manatees, including the possibility that females have false estrous periods. He was also the first to warn that despite legal protection, manatees were still at risk as the result of habitat alteration and death caused by powerboat propellers. Hartman recommended that boat speeds be regulated at strategic locations and that marine sanctuaries be established to further protect the endangered animals.

Powell continued studying the Crystal River manatees into the early 1980s as an employee of the Sirenia Project. Ongoing research there has resulted in one of the longest continuous studies of a single manatee population to date. Other manatee research begun in the 1970s included John E. Reynolds's 1974 to 1977 study of manatee herd structure at Blue Lagoon Lake near Miami, and in 1979 Wayne Hartley began

BELOW: *At the bottom of Crystal River, a fish eats algae from the eye area of a manatee. This manatee looks fast asleep—but it is only half-asleep. To prevent drowning, the brain hemispheres of aquatic mammals take turns sleeping (marked by slow brain waves). Half of their brain sleeps while the other half remains awake so the animal can periodically surface to breathe.*

"Aerial surveys are the primary means of obtaining information on manatee distribution and relative abundance in Florida."

❧

—BRUCE ACKERMAN,
biologist,
Florida Department of
Environmental Protection

his labor of love studying the wintering manatees at Blue Spring State Park. During more than 20 years of observation, Hartley has watched the ravages of time—and powerboat propellers—affect the animals he knows like family.

In 1974 the Sirenia Project, based in Gainesville, Florida, was established by the U.S. Fish and Wildlife Service (the project is now part of the U.S. Geological Survey, Biological Resources Division). From the start, its purpose has been to plan and conduct research on the life history and population ecology of free-ranging West Indian manatees in Florida and Puerto Rico. Specific studies have looked at manatee diet, metabolism rates, social behavior, survival, and seasonal migratory patterns, as well as their vocalizations, saltwater-to-freshwater physiology, genetics, and reproduction.

Because manatees and dugongs are the only plant-eating marine mammals in existence today, scientists are interested in learning all they can about the specialized behavior, anatomy, and physiology that make this possible. Ongoing studies of both wild and captive manatees, combined with extensive lab work, have revealed that the sirenians are both unique and vulnerable to extinction, due to their low metabolic rate, slow reproducion, and very specific habitat requirements.

Field biologists began studying manatee behavior and biology 30 years ago on shoestring budgets. Today millions of dollars are spent each year on manatee research and conservation management, involving the collaborative efforts of literally hundreds of people.

Whiskered Submersibles

Manatees are hydrodynamically designed for life in water. Their hind legs and external earlobes have been eliminated, their eyes reduced in size, and their nostrils positioned at the tip of their stubby snouts for surface breathing. They appear neckless, as the only part of the manatee's head that is clearly defined is the snout—mouth, lips, and eyes. The rest of the head is engulfed by the manatee's ever widening blimplike body. Elongated and swollen in the middle but with tapered ends, sirenians have what is called a fusiform body shape, one that is ideal for swimming.

Even their internal anatomy reflects their aquatic lifestyle. For example, their flattened, 3-foot-long lungs lie horizontally along their backbone instead of in association with the rib cage (as is true for terrestrial mammals). This design creates a straight line from the nostrils, positioned at the tip of the snout, to the lungs, which aids in surface breathing and buoyancy control.

Another unusual anatomical feature has to do with the diaphragm—manatees have not one, but two. Each lung is located in a separate cavity with its own half-width diaphragm, which suggests that the lungs function independently of each other. By relaxing and contracting the muscles in their diaphragms and rib cage, manatees adjust the volume of air in their lungs to achieve neutral buoyancy. This enables the half-ton animals to walk effortlessly along the bottom of waterways, hover motionless in the water column, and float to the surface to breathe with hardly a movement—leaving but a small ripple to mark the spot where their nostrils break the surface.

Author Tim Dietz encountered a dozing manatee resting on the sandy bottom of Kings Bay. The animal's eyes were closed, flippers pulled in close to its sides, and broad tail tucked slightly under. As Dietz watched, the manatee stayed in this position for about four or five minutes before opening its eyes, gently arching its back, then rising to the surface for a breath of air—all with hardly a muscle movement. After refilling its lungs at the surface, the sleepy mammal quietly sank back to the bottom to resume resting with its snout buried in the sand—an enviable demonstration of buoyancy control and total relaxation.

Because of their anatomy, manatees cannot breathe through their mouths, only through their nostrils. This enables them to feed underwater on aquatic plants without getting water into their lungs. While submerged, their nostrils shut tight with muscular flaps like hatches on a submarine, and a protective membrane closes over their eyes. The nostrils open only when a manatee surfaces to breathe; at all other times, the animal remains effectively airtight.

Sirenian Bones

Not surprising for a half-ton animal, manatee bones are dense and heavy. The ribs and the long bones of the forelimbs lack marrow cavities. This rocklike density has helped their ivory-like bones survive intact in the fossil record. Sadly, it also attests to the violent nature of the bone-snapping injuries manatees endure when hit by barges and

"In the 1970s, popular and technical publications may well have given the impression that the common name of the animal was not simply 'manatee' but 'the poorly studied manatee.' That situation changed. Unanswered questions remain, but important databases now exist."

☙

—JOHN E. REYNOLDS,
chairman, U.S. Marine Mammal Commission

In the Company of Manatees

high-speed powerboats. The heavy pachyostotic (marrowless) bones, set lower in the body, undoubtedly serve as ballast to help offset the manatee's positive buoyancy created by its modest blubber and fat, large lungs, and the perpetual production of intestinal gas with plant digestion. With so many of the major bones lacking marrow, red blood cells are probably produced by the liver and in the marrow found in the lighter-weight, more porous backbone and sternum.

Manatees appear neckless for a good reason. While most mammals, including giraffes, have seven cervical (neck) vertebrae, manatees have only six. This explains why their heads seem to disappear right into their bodies, and why manatees cannot turn their heads from side to side. In order to look behind them, they must turn their whole body using their tail and flippers.

Evidence of the manatees' terrestrial past can be found by looking at their pelvic bones, which no longer attach to their backbones but still show a vestigial trace of the hind limbs that degenerated millions of years ago. Located in tissue near the reproductive organs and bladder, the pelvic bones are soft at birth but eventually harden as a manatee matures. As is true of all ungulates, the collarbones are missing entirely.

Undoubtedly some of the more interesting bones in a manatee's body are those found in its flippers. Similar in design to that of a human hand, the jointed and elon-

OPPOSITE: *A manatee's ability to survive depends on clear air passages and access to the surface to breathe. South American hunters exploited this vulnerability by stuffing wooden pegs into the animals' nostrils.*

BELOW: *Manatees achieve neutral buoyancy by changing the amount of air in their three-foot-long lungs. This enables them to hang motionless in the water, rest like logs on the bottom, and move up or down in the water column with little movement or energy expenditure.*

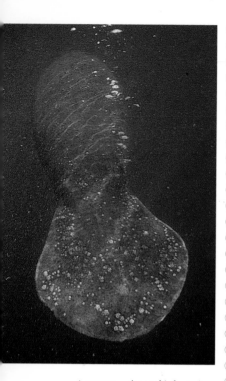

ABOVE: *Anaerobic bacteria help manatees break down their plant food (cellulose) through fermentation. Methane gas is often a telltale by-product of this slow digestive process.*

"To watch a manatee glide upside down or perform rolls, somersaults, head and tail stands is akin to watching an underwater ballet, so fluid and effortless are the motions."

༄

—TIM DIETZ,
in The Call of the Siren

gated "finger bones" help the animals hold food to their mouths; scull through the water; grasp ropes, anchor lines, and each other; and "walk" on their flippered "finger-tips" along the bottom of waterways.

Locomotion

Manatee locomotion is slow and contemplative. These giants move through the water propelled by graceful up-and-down motions of their paddle-shaped tails. With the slightest change in angle, their tails also serve as sensitive rudders. At the front end, manatee flippers are used as steering aids, for lateral movements, and for "walking."

During the day, manatees can sometimes be seen in small groups at the surface, often swimming in single file. They typically cruise at relaxed speeds of 2 to 3 mph, but if threatened they can press their flippers to their sides and use their tails to generate bursts of speed up to 15 mph. "They may seem fat, dumpy and flaccid," wrote author M. Timothy O'Keefe, "but manatees are actually very muscular animals."

Despite their swollen proportions (and ungainly efforts to partly haul out of the water to reach shoreline vegetation), manatees are extremely agile. By exploiting the gravity-defying properties of water to achieve neutral buoyancy, they move gracefully, almost ghostlike, through their aquatic habitat. In fact, like their elephant relatives on land, manatees move so unobtrusively that many a scuba diver has been startled to find a manatee's bulbous snout suddenly appear just inches from their faceplate.

Enjoying the three-dimensional freedom of life spent in a liquid, manatees do somersaults, barrel rolls, head and tail stands, and half gainers—all in slow motion—as they serenely glide along, often upside down. Many of their movements appear comical, if not joyful, as the curious mammals explore and manipulate their environment, including each other, with their whiskered lips and dextrous flippers.

"Despite the manatee's weird appearance," wrote M. Timothy O'Keefe in *Manatees: Our Vanishing Mermaids,* "there is still something majestic, almost regal, in the way these animals move and act. They move slowly, never appearing to be in any hurry. But with just a couple flips of their tail, they can outdistance the fastest swimmer."

The Eyes of a Mermaid

Manatees have remarkably small eyes in comparison to their bulky body size—another adaptation for life underwater. Their lidless orbs are well developed and the retina contains both cone and rod cells, which indicates that they can probably see in bright (cones) and dim light (rods), as well as in color. Despite the limited visibility permitted through water, manatees seem to have fairly good eyesight. When tested, they responded to visual cues held 115 feet away and could distinguish between objects of different size, color, and pattern. Studies of eye anatomy and spectral sensitivity in Amazonian manatees revealed that they have some binocularity and can produce a well-focused image underwater.

ABOVE: *Manatees have favorite play objects, which they return to year after year, such as this submerged palm tree at Blue Spring.*

LEFT: *Another manatee uses the same tree trunk as a scratching post. Blue Spring manatees play with just about everything in their water habitat, including the occasional dozing alligator.*

Manatee eye muscles close in a circular motion, much like the aperture on a camera. As a result, the animals have a starburst of crow's-feet that encircle their eyes. These subtle character lines add an inquisitive warmth to their innocent facial expression. In contrast, the protective nictitating membrane that closes over each eye when the manatee dives often gives these creatures an eerie white-eyed appearance that makes them look like they are either blind or dead.

Invisible Ears

Despite the absence of external ears (a nearly invisible ear opening is located behind each eye), manatees do have an excellent sense of hearing. Indeed, so proverbial is a manatee's ability to detect sounds underwater that in the Amazon region, human parents often adorn their infants with charms made from manatee ear bones so they will grow up to "hear like a manatee."

Edmund Gerstein, director of marine mammal research at Florida Atlantic University, has demonstrated that manatees have a hearing range of 400 Hz to 46 kHz, with an optimal range between 16 to 18 kHz. His research has shown that manatees have a much greater sensitivity to higher-frequency sounds than was commonly thought.

Keen auditory abilities are important to social animals like the manatee that often travel through turbid water with limited visibility. To maintain contact with each other,

OPPOSITE: *Most mammals have seven vertebrae. Manatees have only six, which explains why they appear neckless, and cannot move their heads from side to side. In order to look behind them, they must move their entire body.*

BELOW: *Manatees often "walk" along the bottom of shallow waterways on the tips of their flippers.*

manatees produce a series of chirps, squeals, and whistles. These vocalizations are especially crucial between mother-calf pairs, whose strong bond and close physical contact is maintained through an exchange of vocal "pings" that signal each other's location. Females have been observed responding to their calf's call from 200 feet.

Other indications that hearing is very important to manatees are the large ear bones, which are well developed at birth, and the enlarged areas of the brain associated with hearing. Because their ear openings are so small, and their ear canals appear closed, manatees probably receive sound signals differently than terrestrial mammals do. Scientists have proposed that the manatees' large cheekbones (which abut their ear bones) may, in fact, be their main area of sound reception. A similar sound system exists in dolphins, whose fat-filled lower jaws conduct sound to their ear bones.

According to John E. Reynolds, anatomical studies suggest that manatees are adapted to hear infrasonic frequencies that are too low (20 Hz or less) to be heard by the human ear. However, such sounds do not travel well in shallow water. Gerstein's research has demonstrated that manatees do not actually hear these frequencies. At close distances they *feel* the infrasonic frequencies through vibral-tactile sensations transmitted through the sensory hairs located all over their bodies.

"Manatees have excellent hearing for the shallow-water environments in which they live," says Gerstein. "Unfortunately, boats, which produce low-frequency sounds, were never part of their evolutionary environment."

Intelligence

"When I first started working with manatees," says photographer Jeff Foott, "not much had been done with them, and they weren't given much credit for intelligence. But I had an experience with them in the wild that proved just how smart they really are. While diving with a mother-calf pair at Crystal River, I watched as the female fed on hydrilla—a very stringy plant, much like spaghetti. A piece of the plant got stuck in the female's gums and I watched as she tried and tried to dislodge it with her flippers while contorting her mouth and lips into every possible position. Finally, after five or six minutes without success, she swam straight to my boat's anchor line and used it like dental floss to clean the plant right out of her mouth. It was then that I first realized manatees are a lot smarter than they are given credit for, and that the female's behavior showed not only conscious thought and decision making but even tool use."

Throughout history, people have equated the manatees' roly-poly girth and slow, contemplative movements with a lack of intelligence. How could such a big, wild animal be so tame and trusting, if not stupid? Such assumptions, reflected in the nickname "sea cows," probably made it easier to butcher the defenseless mammals for meat, lamp oil, and leather, and to justify the cruelty of outright abuse. But it turns out that manatees are far from stupid, even if their brains are small for their body size.

According to University of Wisconsin neurophysiologist Wallace Welker, the brain of an adult manatee is about the size of a softball. When compared with a brain of

"Despite its clumsy appearance and expressionless face, the manatee is not quite so stupid as is generally supposed."

—GEORGE GOODWIN, *in* The Animal Kingdom, *1954*

"One day a female manatee seemed to be fascinated with our boat. She would swim slowly around and nuzzle the stern or rub herself on our anchor rope. She was such a friendly animal that we wanted an appropriate name for her. We asked Junji for a name in Japanese that would be suitable. He suggested 'Tomo,' which is a short form of the Japanese word for "friend."

—ALAN HICKENBOTTOM, *Earthwatch Team Member, Florida Manatees Project*

comparable size, such as that of domestic cattle, the manatee's cerebral cortex appears relatively smooth and unfissured. Welker believes that this indicates that manatee brains have fewer and less varied cortical regions—which, in turn, is reflected in their relatively simple perceptual and behavioral repertoires, and gentle temperament.

However, Roger Reep, professor and supervisor of the University of Florida Manatee Research Group, believes that the low brain-to-body weight ratio found in sirenians probably has more to do with selection for large body size as an adaptation to aquatic herbivory than with a reduction of cognitive potential (29 distinct cortical areas have been identified so far). "Perhaps because of their relaxed lifestyle and low brain-body weight ratios," says Reep, "it is commonly assumed that manatees possess limited cognitive capacity. However, their abilities may be hidden by our prejudice in favor of fast-moving, visually dominant animals."

Manatees at the Miami Seaquarium have demonstrated good memory and hearing abilities by bobbing to the surface when their individual names are called. In the 1980s, psychologist Dale Woodyard of the University of Windsor in Ontario, Canada, demonstrated that manatees have reasoning ability when he trained captive manatees to choose a large circle over a small one in order to obtain a carrot reward, then reversed the reward prerequisite over and over again. The manatees learned within one wrong choice when the game had switched.

Working with the manatees at Tampa's Lowry Park Zoo, biologist Edmund Gerstein and his wife, Laura, found that manatees can learn complex discrimination tasks as quickly and easily as dolphins, and even faster than seals and sea lions. At Lowry Park, the Gersteins taught two manatees named Dundee and Stormy to swim, on cue, to a listening hoop, place their heads inside, and wait for a computerized tone to be played, or not played, underwater. Each manatee then had to leave the hoop and select a "yes" or "no" panel, indicating whether or not they had heard the sound.

Through their experiments, the Gersteins have demonstrated which sounds manatees can and cannot hear. They have also shown that manatees have excellent short-term and long-term memory: After a four-year hiatus from the project, when tested again, both Stormy and Dundee remembered the complex visual and acoustic relationships they had learned several years earlier.

"Stormy has helped dispel the belief that manatees are dull-witted and so are unable to avoid dangerous boat situations," says Gerstein, "when, in fact, they can make cognitive choices and learn quickly."

If manatees can learn, remember, and move quickly when in danger (about 21 feet per second), then why are they repeatedly hit by boats? The Gersteins' research indicates that boat noise is on the fringe of the animals' lower frequency range. As a result, manatees have trouble sensing boats at safe distances. When a vessel gets close enough to be detected, it is usually too late for the manatee to react in time.

Aquatic Plant Eaters

Manatees and dugongs, like elephants, are nonruminant herbivores. They eat plants. In fact, as previously noted, the sirenians are the only plant-eating marine mammals alive today. (African hippopotamuses are aquatic and eat plants, but they live in water by day to avoid overheating and graze on land at night.) Marine sea turtles eat plants and share habitat with sirenians, but they are reptiles, not mammals.

Because their diet is primarily of low-quality cellulose, manatees must eat large quantities in order to obtain adequate energy and nutrition. This explains why they have been nicknamed "eating machines" and "sea cows." Grazing up to eight hours a day, they can consume 10 to 15 percent of their body weight in food each day.

Plant material is hard to digest. To facilitate the slow digestive process required to

BELOW: *A manatee demonstrates how it uses its prehensile upper lips, lined with stiff, white, perioral bristles, to manipulate its food—in this case, a water hyacinth.*

break down their bulky high-fiber, low-protein diet, manatees have long intestines—up to 130 feet in length. Through fermentation, resident anaerobic bacteria in the hindgut break down the plant cellulose. This symbiotic arrangement with the bacteria, coupled with the manatees' vast intestinal plumbing, enables the animals to process huge quantities of plant food. To protect the lining of the digestive system from abrasion, a large cardiac or digestive gland coats the food items with mucus as they pass through the stomach.

Energy Conservation

"As travelers in the slow lane of life," wrote Mark Walters *(Reader's Digest,* August 1985), "the manatees have collected some peculiar traits. Day after day, while other animals fight for survival, the manatees while away their time like vacationing sumo wrestlers. Eating, sleeping, lolling in the shadows, they are oblivious to the fish nibbling at their coarse hides—mobile homes to barnacles and parasites."

Couch potatoes take note: Dugongs and manatees are champions when it comes to energy conservation—they expend as little of it as possible unless absolutely necessary. In fact, scientists have calculated that manatees expend about one-third the energy required for a mammal of comparable size.

Having evolved in an environment devoid of humans, manatees have little need for speed. By living predominantly in tropical and subtropical waters, where less energy is needed to regulate body temperature, manatees could afford to slow down their metabolic rate—and they did. It turns out that a slow metabolic rate, coupled with large body size, is a highly adaptive strategy in the evolutionary arms race between herbivores in competition for plant food. For a given digestive system, differences in metabolic rate enable a large animal to feed on less nutritious plant parts, but more of them, and thus compete with smaller animals that can afford to eat less of more nutritious leaf shoots and fruits. For example, elephants compete with the smaller, more abundant terrestrial herbivores, succeeding through sheer size, their reduced metabolic rate, and their ability to feed on the woody parts of trees and shrubs, which other mammalian herbivores can neither reach nor digest. The sirenia went one step further. They took to the sea, leaving behind their terrestrial competition to fill the niche of the "only plant-eating marine mammals."

When they aren't feeding, Florida manatees typically spend the day dozing and digesting. To conserve oxygen (and energy), their normal heart rate of 50 to 60 beats per minute slows to 30 beats per minute when they dive. At rest, they can remain submerged for up to 20 minutes, but they usually surface to breathe every 3 to 4 minutes—every 30 seconds if they are expending a great deal of energy. Dozing motionless on the bottom of shallow waterways, they seem oblivious to the fish that school around them, attracted by the edible algae on their skin. At times the only visible movement from the resting behemoths is the intermittent release of gas bubbles that race to the surface—an unavoidable by-product of plant digestion.

"If manatees kept their schedules on those little organizers that business-persons are always consulting, a typical working day might look like this: 10 A.M. to 2:14 P.M.—float; 2:15 to 2:17 P.M.—emit three to four blooping, aromatic bubbles of manatee gas; 2:18 P.M. to dusk—continue floating."

— DAVE BARRY

Social Behavior

"They kept diving and regrouping, mouthing and rubbing each other and barrel-rolling," wrote Nini Block *(Earthwatch,* November 1993). "I hadn't expected such a party atmosphere from mammals that the literature described as 'generally solitary animals,' whose only strong bonds formed between mother and calf. These were clearly social animals that, like elephants, loved physical contact and play."

Unlike most animals, manatees are not territorial. They do not fight over mates or real estate. Instead, these gentle, nonaggressive mammals playfully chase, bump, and bodysurf together; grab each other's flippers; and mouth one another with their big mobile lips, appearing to "kiss" each other in greeting.

Lacking natural enemies, Florida manatees do not need to travel in large herds for protection. Only during the cold winter months do they congregate together in substantial numbers at the limited warm-water refuges in Florida. The rest of the year they disperse, traveling solo or in small, transitory groups of two or three individuals.

The mother-calf pair is by far the strongest and longest-lasting manatee relationship. Juvenile males also form bachelor herds that persist for prolonged periods of time. In general, manatee groups lack a defined structure as well as a specific leader. Only during the formation of mating herds, consisting of 5 to 22 males, is there a group focus—on the single estrous female around which the males have gathered.

ABOVE: *When not feeding, playing, or traveling, manatees spend a lot of time simply dozing—sideways, upside down, or with their muzzles resting in the bottom sediment.*

FOLLOWING PAGES: *Manatees are nonagressive. They do not defend territories, nor are they able to bite. They socialize with each other through touch and vocalizations.*

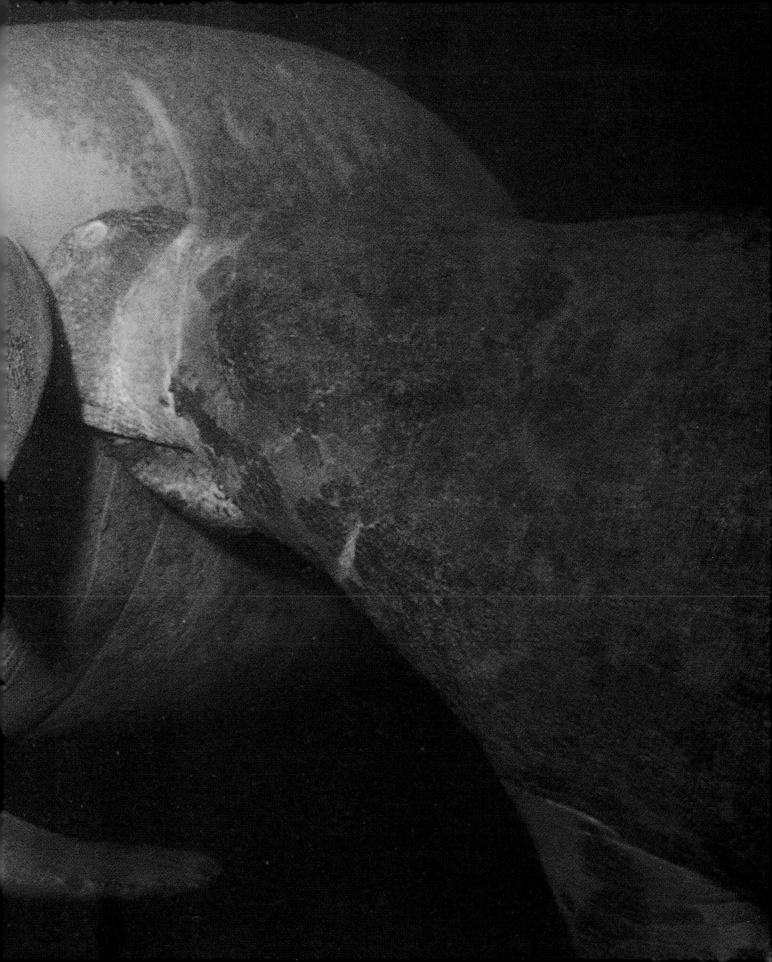

RIGHT: *Methane gas bubbles from a plant-eating manatee catch the sunlight.*

BELOW: *A manatee mom and calf demonstrate the agile use of their flippers to scull and steer as they swim in Crystal River.*

Manatees are far more social than scientists originally suspected. They can be seen breathing, turning, and diving in unison as they swim together single file. They doze in body contact at the bottom of spring runs. A few even enjoy the company of people.

"They are very curious animals," says Gerstein of his work with captive manatees. "Whenever anything goes into the water, they come right over to investigate it with their whiskers. There is no feeling quite like being gummed by a manatee."

Tactile Behavior

Typical of many marine mammals, manatees are extremely tactile. They nuzzle each other affectionately snout to snout, appear to "kiss" each other in greeting, embrace one another with their flippers, and swim in loosely synchronized formations—single file or next to each other. It is not uncommon to see manatees dozing together at the bottom of shallow waterways in quiet, motionless physical contact—a flipper touching a back, tails touching tails.

In 1998, scientists at the University of Bonn in Germany reported that seals can detect fish in murky water by using their whiskers to sense tiny water movements. Although other aquatic animals are known to have such motion-sensing systems, this was the first description of such a system in marine mammals. Manatees not only have sensory hairs covering their upper lips but also 1- to 2-inch-long sensory hairs scattered over the surface of their bodies. These hairs are probably used to detect the slightest water movements, as well as the proximity of objects underwater and the enjoyable touch of their tactile manatee companions.

Manatees use their tails, flippers, bodies, and prehensile lips to make physical contact with each other. They are covered with sensitive rubbery skin that is ideal for such touchy-feely contact. Manatee moms occasionally embrace their calves with their flippers. At Crystal River, a few manatees even do the same to scuba divers, while others approach boats to get back rubs. "You can tell when you've become friends with a manatee," says Timothy O'Keefe. "He'll nudge you to have you scratch his head, or do a barrel roll and stand on his head so you can scratch his stomach. I've had many follow me around and almost demand to be petted or scratched. Once you've gained an animal's confidence, it may follow you around like a puppy."

Play Behavior

Manatees are playful, joyful creatures. They bodysurf in floodgates, do barrel rolls, and swim upside down. When John E. Reynolds studied a group of 50 manatees in Blue Lagoon Lake, he discovered that not only were his subjects sociable but that they liked to have fun. They went joyriding on the strong currents below flood-control structures and played "follow-the-leader" near barges.

Anyone who has worked with manatees reports that their individual personalities are often as distinct as our own—and characters there are many. Take, for example, the

"I came to Crystal River with a firm resolve to abide by all the rules. But I forgot to tell the manatees of my plans. Down there they set the rules, and I quickly found out that if they want to use you for a scratching post, you have no say in the matter."

☙

—TIM DIETZ,
in The Call of the Siren

IN THE COMPANY OF MANATEES

LEFT: *While surfacing to breathe, a manatee exposes the business end of this plant-eating marine mammal. Manatees eat more than 60 different kinds of plants. Notice the split upper lips, used to grab vegetation.*

OPPOSITE, TOP LEFT: *With nostrils sealed shut and flippers held close, a manatee momentarily rests on its side. Many of their movements appear joyful as the animals gracefully glide and barrel-roll through the water.*

OPPOSITE, TOP RIGHT: *A Crystal River manatee takes time out for an upside-down back scratch.*

OPPOSITE, BELOW: *Manatees are social, tactile animals. They nuzzle each other with their lips, and make gentle contact with their flippers and tails.*

manatee that regularly showed up at a marina in Miami to have its belly scratched with a deck brush. St. Augustine had a similar mascot—a large manatee that routinely visited the dockmaster at the city yacht pier to have him scrape the barnacles off its back with a paint scraper.

At Tampa's Lowry Park Zoo, a manatee named J.P. grabbed the legs of his diver/keeper and pulled her underwater so they were eye to eye. Another manatee named Buffett crawled over a Plexiglas partition so that he could swim and play with his manatee neighbors. Probably the funniest manatee at the zoo's Manatee Center is Dundee, who follows his keepers around to grab excess lettuce and begs for food by tapping his mouth with his right flipper as he floats at the surface.

At Blue Spring State Park, where researchers often perch in trees overhanging the run to spy on manatee behavior, ranger Wayne Hartley has amassed 20 years of amusing anecdotes about manatee play behavior. Take, for instance, Phud, a young male who likes to lie sideways on the bottom of Blue Spring and let the current roll him over and over down the run. "Normally the only time you see manatees do this is when they are sick," says Hartley.

A female manatee named Lily routinely approached swimmers unless she had a calf. Then she was conflicted—she wanted to play with people but keep her calf at a safe distance. "I could hear the photographers laughing through their snorkels," says Hartley, "as Lily tried unsuccessfully to do both in a game of 'do as I say, not as I do' with her calf. Manatees will play with anything. I've watched them play tug-of-war and games of keep-away. Sometimes it's hard to get ropes out of the water before they get all wrapped up in them. Once I had to jump into the water to get a manatee loose from a piling."

Then there is Georgia, the park's "problem child." Rescued as a 60-pound calf in Georgia and raised in captivity at SeaWorld Orlando until she weighed 1,600 pounds, this affectionate manatee has been a lovable pest ever since she was released at Blue Spring. "She likes people so much," says Hartley, "that she goes right into the swimmers-only area to be with them, hugging them, pulling them underwater, and chasing them up the steps to grab their legs with her flippers if they try to leave."

When Save the Manatee Club staffer Pat Rose finished photographing her one day and turned his underwater lens toward the other manatees in the run, jealous Georgia did a series of barrel rolls right across the swimming area, hitting him in the shoulder. With such antics continuing into the early summer, Georgia finally wore out her welcome and was captured and relocated 20 miles away from Blue Spring in an area she was already very familiar with. Apparently, it wasn't far enough, says Hartley, as Georgia was recently spotted just 3 miles from the park—with a calf—heading their way.

"We want her back," says Hartley, "just not all year long."

Just as manatees use anchor chains and ropes like dental floss to dislodge plant material stuck in their mouths, a few seem to view snorkelers and divers in the same utilitarian light—as ready-made play objects, and a good source for back rubs and belly scratches. Aware of this, one scuba diver brought along a small plastic brush that fit in

"At play, manatees touch muzzle to muzzle in what can best be described as a kiss. This behavior is one facet of a whole repertoire of nuzzles, nibbles, nudges, butts, and embraces. The performance as a whole becomes a serene ballet, a slow-motion ritual of lazy posturings and positionings, twistings, and turnings. This intimate activity is not necessarily performed in a sexual context; calves participate with adults, as do subadults with other adolescents of the same sex."

❧

—DANIEL HARTMAN, *in* Ecology and Behavior of the Manatee in Florida

ABOVE: *Using its flippers like hands, a manatee holds tight to the end of a submerged palm tree in Blue Spring Run.*

LEFT: *An inquisitive, tactile manatee uses its perioral bristles and prehensile lips to gum on a submerged log.*

the palm of her hand—all the better to please the massage-seeking manatees that approached her at Crystal River.

"Manatee calves are incredibly playful," adds photographer Jeff Foott. "They are always looking for an opportunity to play—with each other and everything around them. I've seen a calf intentionally harass a school of fish, swimming in and out of it and chasing the fish just to bug them. I've also watched manatee calves poke at blue crabs, apparently amused by their response."

Vocalizations

In the *Odyssey,* Homer described the song of the sirens as being so irresistible that Ulysses' crew filled their ears with warm beeswax to avoid being lured onto the rocks by the bewitching songsters. Ulysses, however, insisted on hearing the songs—but first had his crew lash him to the ship's mast so he wouldn't lead them all to their doom.

Now fast-forward to present-day Florida, to the underwater observation room at Homosassa Springs State Wildlife Park, which is located just south of Crystal River on the west coast. Here visitors can watch the slow-motion, underwater antics of the park's resident manatees through thick glass as the animals "walk" along the bottom of the spring run, expel lazy gas bubbles, and wrestle heads of lettuce with their dextrous flippers and bristled lips. Underwater microphones, positioned near the floating wooden feeding frames used to corral the lettuce, make it possible to eavesdrop on these roly-poly herbivores.

Just how alluring are the songs of the sirens? During my visit to Homosassa Springs, a continuous stream of whistle-squeaks, chirps, and squeals (small sounds for such robust animals) poured through the speakers into the underwater observation room. Such lighthearted vocalizations could never lure anyone to their doom—not even a slap-happy sailor. Scientists have proposed that the manatee's full vocal repertoire ranges between 400 Hz and 16 kHz. However, Gerstein along with Navy scientists has recently recorded manatee vocalizations ranging from 400 Hz to 36 kHz. Only at Homosassa is it possible to have such an unforgettable surround-sound manatee experience while viewing the animals eye-to-eye underwater—no scuba tanks or snorkels required.

John Morris and Cathy Steel of the Florida Institute of Technology discovered that manatees have a unique vocabulary that includes many different distinct sounds. They communicate with each other through a series of one-syllable squeaks, chirps, and squeals, producing sounds that convey mood, sexual information, and warnings. They vocalize when they are courting and playing, and they "talk" faster and at a rising pitch when they sense danger. They even groan when they stretch.

Manatees use their vocalizations to maintain contact with one another as they move through the water, especially when the animals are feeding or traveling in turbid water. Not surprising, Morris and Steel found that vocalizations between mother and calf are the most frequent. When a floodgate separated a mother and calf for three hours in Florida, the two animals vocalized (dueted) constantly until they were reunited.

Years ago photographer Jeff Foott experienced the social, vocal nature of Florida's manatees firsthand while filming them at Crystal River. At the start of the shoot, Jeff selected a mother and calf that he could work with each day. The pair eventually became habituated to him, going about their normal dozing and plant-munching activities as he filmed. At the end of the winter season, the weather suddenly got warm, and Jeff, and the manatees, left the refuge. Jeff relocated to the Everglades to continue filming. However, a few weeks later a fluke cold snap occurred, and he decided to return to Crystal River to see if any manatees had retreated to the warm-water refuge. Sure enough, there was the same mother-calf pair he had befriended earlier. Upon seeing Jeff, the calf got so excited that he swam up, grabbed Jeff's arm with his flipper, and enthusiastically began to chirp and squeak.

Teeth

The West Indian manatee has five to seven exposed low-crowned cheek teeth in each jaw, located toward the rear of the mouth. In appearance, the teeth have been compared to those of people—and pigs—yet that is where the similarity ends. With the exception of the few teeth that erupt before or soon after birth (similar to our deciduous premolars), all of a manatee's adult teeth are grinding molars that are continuously replaced during the animal's lifetime. The molars form at the back of the jaw, wear down as they migrate forward, and eventually fall out. The horizontal forces generated while chewing push the tooth row forward. By the time a worn-out tooth reaches the front of the row and is lost, it has already been replaced by a newly erupted, fully rooted tooth at the rear.

Anatomical and behavioral studies of Amazonian manatees conducted at the Instituto Nacional de Pesquisas da Amazonia (INPA) revealed how the animals have adapted to eat-

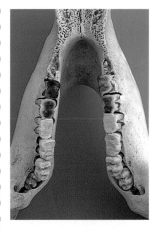

ABOVE: *Grinding molars, located in the back of their mouths, grow continuously during a manatee's lifetime. As each tooth erupts from the back of the jaw, it moves forward to eventually replace the worn tooth that falls out in front.*

ing a diet of aquatic plants that typically float above their heads. INPA scientists recovered the teeth shed by their captive subjects and measured the rate of replacement. They found that on average, a manatee's teeth move forward about 1 millimeter per month but that this rate varies based on the quality and quantity of food chewed by each animal.

Such a system of perpetually moving, rejuvenating teeth is the perfect adaptation for a half-ton marine mammal that must dine on and grind enormous quantities of abrasive plant material. In South America, many of the grasses that form large floating mats in the rivers contain silica, an abrasive defense against herbivores. In fact, silica causes rapid tooth wear. The manatee's conveyor-belt teeth make it possible for the animals to eat these and other high-fiber, low-protein plants, filling a specialized dietary niche that separates the Sirenia (manatees and dugongs) from all other marine mammals—all of which eat meat, not plants.

Pacifist Plant Eaters

BELOW: *A Crystal River manatee uses its flippers, prehensile upper lips, and perioral bristles to subdue a large clump of hydrilla.*

Manatees are the undisputed pacifists of the animal kingdom. "They own no threatening gestures—no displays of teeth (they're toothless except for big, grinding molars in the back) and no loud roars (they let out only timid squeaks and whistles)," wrote Mark Walters in *Reader's Digest* (August 1985).

Manatees do not fight for food, nor do they defend territories. They can't even bite. Considering the thousands of people who have swum with (and frequently harassed) manatees at Crystal River without incident, manatees have proved their docility. A young woman at Blue Spring once had a manatee roll on her, momentarily pinning her to the bottom of the run when her flipper got caught under the animal—but this was accidental and brief. Lacking any system of defense, when frightened or harassed, manatees simply disappear with the flip of their tails.

"Manatees give the appearance of being docile," says Daniel Odell of SeaWorld Orlando, "but I've seen them, in captivity, flip a 200-pound man into the air with their tails if aggravated."

According to Blue Spring ranger Wayne Hartley, the standard rule when handling captive manatees is "never let them get on their back." If you're in a truck with them when they do, everyone knows to get out fast, says Hartley. Under such stressful conditions, where the body weight of the manatee is pressing down on its lungs, Hartley has seen manatees take aim with their tails. Such an occurrence is rare, however, as under normal conditions, manatees are not drydocked on their backs, and they normally lie very still as soon as they realize they are stranded.

Feeding Behavior

Manatee mouths are designed to munch. The animals' mobile upper lips are split down the middle and move independently of each other to pull plants into their mouths. The lips are covered with whiskers (sensory hairs called vibrissae). Each is separately attached to its own nerve endings and blood supply. Manatees use their sensitive lips (equivalent to the tip of an elephant's trunk) like hands. Horny, ridged pads located at the front of the upper and lower jaws help to grasp and crush the plant material en route to the grinding molars.

Until recently, not much attention was paid to the manatee's very specialized feeding apparatus. Almost invisible, except when everted, are the stiff, white, conical-shaped perioral bristles (made out of fingernail material) that line the inside edges of the upper lips. Daniel Hartman observed that while feeding, a manatee will "evert its horrendous lip pads and tuck the plants into its mouth with the attached bristles." It is now known that seven different facial muscles control the movement of the perioral bristles, and they do this so precisely that a manatee can roll a carrot between its prehensile lips like a person might roll a pencil between their thumb and index finger.

"The appearance produced by the movements of this peculiar organ is very much the same as that of the mouth in the silkworm and other caterpillars whilst devouring a leaf," wrote Richard Lydekker (*The Royal Natural History*, 1894), "the jaws in these insects diverging and converging laterally, in a very similar manner during mastication."

While feeding, manatees often float vertically, using their flippers to pull plants within reach of their oversize lips. They spend considerable time grazing on hydrilla

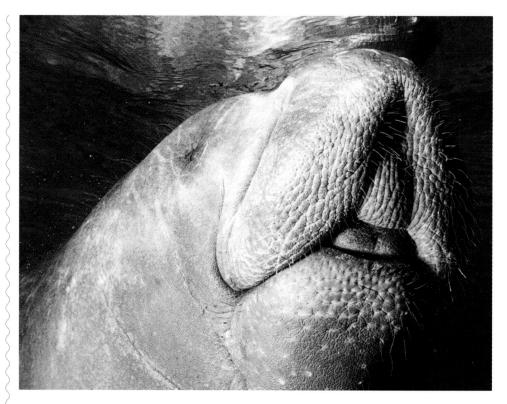

and water hyacinth, two of their favorite foods. They sometimes even haul themselves partially out of the water to consume bank vegetation.

Grazing eight or more hours a day, and chewing two times per second, manatees consume enormous quantities of food each day. The rich microflora that inhabits their enlarged hindguts aids in the slow digestion of cellulose and other fibrous carbohydrates found in their vegetarian diet.

Plants preferred by the West Indian manatee include saltwater species such as manatee grass *(Syringodium filiforme),* shoal grass *(Halodule wrightii),* turtle grass *(Thalassia testudina),* and widgeon grass *(Ruppia maritima).* In freshwater, they eat hydrilla *(Hydrilla verticillata),* water hyacinth *(Eichhornia crassipes),* eelgrass *(Vallisneria neotropicalis),* and water lettuce *(Pistia stratiotes).*

Thomas O'Shea, a former leader of the USGS Sirenia Project, watched manatees wintering in Blue Spring Run forage on acorns that had fallen into the water from the overhanging live oak trees. The resourceful manatees searched fish nests built by male tilapia for acorns—because their circular design made them ideal "collecting bowls" for the felled acorns.

Although primarily herbivorous, manatees ingest numerous invertebrates associated with their plant diet. In captivity, manatees often eat mullet and take their vitamins wrapped in smelt. Jamaican fishermen claim that manatees rob fish from their gill nets, leaving only skeletons behind after they strip away the flesh.

At Blue Spring State Park, ranger Wayne Hartley watched manatees surface "all white around the muzzle" from eating clay. According to Bob Bonde, a biologist with the Sirenia Project, no one really knows why they do this. Possibly the clay provides mineral supplements or is eaten to satisfy hunger when the animals are fasting in response to cold water temperatures. In Brazil local fishermen have reported finding dead manatees after prolonged dry-season entrapment in lakes, their bowels impacted with clay.

Taste and Smell

Although both of these senses have been little studied in sirenians, manatees do have taste buds on the back of their tongues, which indicates that they probably do taste their food. Food-preference studies conducted at Blue Spring State Park showed that manatees actively avoid plants that contain toxins.

Similarly, the presence of olfactory tissue on their small internal nasal bones indicates that manatees can smell, but just how well has not been studied (probably not at all when their nostril valves are shut tight underwater). Scientists have suggested that manatees may use their chemoreceptive abilities (taste and smell) to help recognize each other and to determine when a female is in estrus. Snooty, a 50-year-old captive manatee at Bradenton's South Florida Museum, not only likes perfume but reacts when his keepers change their fragrance.

Manatees have been observed rubbing themselves against rocks, logs, ropes, anchor chains, and the hulls of boats. During Daniel Hartman's study, one crusty old crabber complained that the manatees rubbed on his traps, embedding them so deep in the mud that he couldn't haul them out. Females seem to rub against objects more than males do, using parts of their bodies that produce glandular secretions. While it simply may be a way for the tactile animals to play or to relieve an itch, by rubbing areas around their eyes, chin, and genitals the animals also may be leaving each other chemical messages.

At Blue Spring, Wayne Hartley watched manatees return year after year to rub, mouth, and push around the same submerged trunk of a sabal palm tree. If, as Hartley believes, the manatees are scent-marking when they gather to rub the log, then the site could well serve as an underwater communication switchboard for manatees. On the other hand, the log may simply be one heck of a great scratching post. Florida's manatees show traditional use not only of feeding and wintering areas but of specific objects within those areas.

Metabolism

With such portly proportions, it is hard to imagine that the warm-blooded manatees could have a problem with thermoregulation. Yet they do, because their low metabolic rate makes them better suited for warm water than for cold.

"Manatees are very reptilian in the way they do business," says Scott Wright of the Florida Marine Research Institute. Like those of reptiles, the manatees' daily and seasonal movements are often dictated by external temperature. In cool weather, they seek the warmth of limestone springs and power-plant effluents. As the water temperatures rise, the animals disperse.

Water conducts heat away from the body of a mammal up to 25 times faster than air does, and cold water accelerates the heat loss. This means that marine mammals need a thick layer of blubber, or a higher metabolic rate to counteract the constant loss of body heat to water. Manatees have neither. They have a modest layer of blubber, and fat deposits are found around the intestines and in the muscle tissue.

For the most part, manatee thermoregulation is dependent on external water temperature. During summer, this is not a problem, as water temperatures are generally elevated. But in winter, and during unseasonal cold snaps, manatees often have difficulty producing enough body heat to replace that being lost to cold water. When chilled for prolonged periods of time, manatees become lethargic and stop eating. This response puts them at risk for hypothermia and respiratory disease.

The manatee's precarious temperature balance explains why habitat protection is so critical for this endangered species. Any form of harassment that forces the animals out of their warm-water refuges potentially jeopardizes their ability to survive. This also explains why state and federal laws are in place to prevent such harassment and why enforcement of these laws is taken so seriously.

Special Adaptations

The oxygen-binding capacity of manatee blood is noticeably different from that found in the meat-eating seals and toothed whales that pursue active prey in deep water. Pinnipeds and cetaceans have dark, myoglobin-rich muscles, while manatee muscles have little of this oxygen-storing pigment and vary in color and texture throughout different parts of their body.

Because plants need sunlight for photosynthesis, most aquatic plant species are restricted to relatively shallow depths. This may explain why the plant-eating manatees have only moderate diving capabilities. It is all they need to reach plant food that floats at or near the surface or thrives on the bottom of water shallow enough for penetration by sunlight. The variable color and texture of manatee muscle may also explain why hunters describe the different cuts of manatee meat as tasting like pork, beef, or veal.

Chief Miami Seaquarium veterinarian Dr. Gregory Bossart earned a Ph.D. by studying the immune system of manatees, which he discovered is much more developed in manatees than in other animals. "They have far more lymphocytes and T-helper lymphocytes circulating in their blood system than any other mammal," Dr. Bossart says. "The T-helper lymphocytes [which are the cells attacked by HIV, the AIDS virus, in humans] are responsible for guiding and protecting the whole immune system. Manatees have a tremendous number of T-helper cells circulating in their blood system, which probably explains why they can survive swimming in polluted bodies of water like the Miami River and survive repeated lacerations from boat propellers."

"I like manatees much more than alligators. They inhabit clear, warm water and favor the River Coast for its fresh, hot-water springs surging up through limestone and driving waterways down to the Gulf. Looking into these waterways near the Crystal River, I thought that someone had opened a tap and run off the contents of some giant aquarium, so abundant were the tropical fish and plants."

෴

—CLIVE IRVING, *in* Condé Nast Traveler, *May 1992*

Saltwater to Freshwater Physiology

The Amazonian manatee is the only sirenian that lives entirely in freshwater, while the dugongs are the most marine. In between are the West Indian and West African manatees, which travel freely in and out of both fresh- and saltwater. This raises some interesting questions about the physiology of the latter two species that enables them to do this.

According to the late naturalist Archie Carr, fishes of the world fit loosely into two groups based on their ability to go from saltwater into freshwater and vice versa. Some can make the change habitually; some never or hardly ever do. "A marine fish has blood that is less salty than the water he lives in and so makes certain physiologic moves that keep him from shriveling up because of water loss through osmosis," wrote Carr. "For such a fish to pass quickly into freshwater would confront him with a contrasting danger—that of soaking up water into his cells."

LEFT: *Air bubbles escape from the valved nostrils of a manatee as it rises to the surface to exhale. Although unrelated, the Cetacea (whales, dolphins, and porpoises) and the Sirenia (manatees and dugongs) are the only mammals that spend their entire lives in water.*

Manatees are faced with the same osmotic challenges when they swim from salt- to freshwater and back. Howard Odum, a zoologist at the University of Florida, suggested that the lack of sodium chloride in freshwater may be compensated for by other dissolved solids. For example, dissolved calcium salts are typically found in Florida's limestone spring water. But this wouldn't explain how West African manatees can travel from the Gulf of Guinea 1,250 miles up the Niger River.

Manatee kidneys are flat and lobulated, resembling those of cows rather than the more reniculate kidneys of seals and whales. Although their function has been little studied, their structure suggests the ability to concentrate urine. It has already been shown that manatees living in saltwater produce a more concentrated urine than those living in freshwater—an adaptive step to eliminate the salt taken in with their food and to prevent the additional loss of body fluids to a highly saline environment.

The kidneys of dugongs are cylindrical and more lobulated than those of manatees. Such differences are probably explained by the dugongs' completely marine habitat, which would require the physiological ability to eliminate ingested salt, while conserving body fluids.

Water loss due to osmosis and the need to eliminate ingested salt may explain why Florida manatees must have periodic access to freshwater in order to survive. At the Miami Seaquarium, the animals drink from a pipe running continuous freshwater into their tank. In the wild, Florida manatees congregate at river mouths, sewage outfalls, culverts, and springs. They also seek out freshwater hoses at piers and marinas—a behavior that field biologists sometimes exploit to capture manatees for tagging with radio and satellite transmitters.

Co-Inhabitants

Florida manatees share their water habitat with an amazing assortment of aquatic and semiaquatic creatures, from turtles, river otters, and water snakes to alligators and American crocodiles. Fish school around manatees as they rest on the bottom of shallow waterways, attracted by the veritable feast of algae that grows on their thick wrinkled skin. Green turtles often graze nearby on shared seagrass beds.

According to ranger Wayne Hartley, there is always at least one big alligator in Blue Spring Run with the manatees. "They don't bother each other," says Hartley. "I've watched big adult manatees that are playing roll right over an alligator resting on the bottom, not just once but several times, until the alligator got up and left. I've also seen smaller manatees and calves swim up to alligators and push them with their heads like they would play with each other."

Alligators leave manatees alone, says Hartley, because even a 60-pound calf is too big for them to swallow, and they can't chew their food. They have to wait until a carcass rots before they can tear out bite-size chunks of meat to gulp. Hartley also points out that since manatees lack necks to grab on to, alligators probably haven't figured out how to drown one.

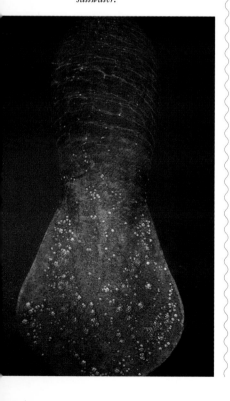

BELOW: *This manatee was photographed in a freshwater river, yet the barnacles on his skin are evidence that he has spent considerable time in saltwater.*

LEFT: *An American alligator floats next to a Florida manatee. Both species generally ignore each other—unless a manatee decides to turn one of the reptiles into an unwilling playmate. Then the gator will flee. (Photo courtesy the Florida Department of Environmental Protection)*

Jeff Foott witnessed a manatee-alligator encounter in Everglades National Park. A manatee was being translocated from up north to the warmth of the park's Flamingo area. Jeff planned to photograph the release, but it was too late in the evening, too dark to take pictures. When they arrived at Flamingo with the manatee in tow, a large alligator was floating off the dock. They tried to encourage the big old gator to leave the area, but the huge reptile wouldn't be intimidated. Jeff helped the biologists carry the half-ton manatee out of the truck.

"No sooner did the manatee touch water," says Jeff, "than the alligator began to chase it, not so much attracted to the manatee itself as to the radio tag floating from the base of its tail. The big gator bit at the float several times, but it remained securely attached."

Apparently, this was not an isolated incident. According to Sirenia Project biologist Bob Bonde, an alligator pulled a transmitter off a manatee in Banana Creek and carried the housing over an earthen dike. Alligators have left their teeth marks on the transmitter housings of tagged manatees in the upper Banana River and Banana Creek in Brevard County. In fact, alligator predation on floating transmitters may have accounted for the loss of signals from several tagged manatees in these areas commonly shared with alligators, says Bonde.

Seasonal Migration Patterns

"It is the nature of wild animals to move ... the endless quest for food, a mate and shelter pushes the animal through its paces," wrote William Stolzenburg, associate editor of *Nature Conservancy* magazine.

In the Company of Manatees

With the onset of cool autumn weather, West Indian manatees seek warm-water refuges in Florida to pass the winter months. Numerous manatee areas have been identified through aerial surveys, VHF (very high frequency) radio tracking, and the use of satellites to monitor the animals' movements. Several of the manatee areas in Florida are warmed by natural artesian springs. The rest are artificially warmed by effluents from power plants and factories. Should a power plant temporarily shut down or reduce its output during a cold front, large numbers of animals could perish. Juveniles are particularly sensitive to cold because of their smaller size. At present, no data show whether the effluents themselves harm the animals.

According to Sirenia Project biologist Jim Reid, most manatees return to the same warm-water refuges each year. Some use different refuges in different years, and others use two or more refuges in the same winter. Many individuals show site fidelity, with specific stopover and feeding areas, including lesser-known, minor aggregation sites used as temporary thermal refuges. The latter are usually canals or boat basins where warmer water temperatures persist as temperatures in nearby bays and rivers drop.

Long-term tracking studies have revealed that manatees along the Atlantic Coast often migrate seasonally between the St. Johns River and southern Florida. When they do, they follow the same migration routes that their mothers and grandmothers did, returning to the same areas year after year. And thanks to the well-publicized wanderings of Chessie the manatee (see below) up and down the East Coast, it is now known that manatees can also make long seasonal migrations of 1,200 miles or more.

But not all manatees travel such great distances. "People have the idea that manatees leave Blue Spring and rush out to the ocean," says park ranger Wayne Hartley, "but they don't. Most remain in the St. Johns River during spring and summer; a few hardly travel more than six miles away from Blue Spring Run."

Chessie the Wandering Manatee

In 1994 an adult male manatee dubbed Chessie suddenly became an instant celebrity when he broke all existing known manatee records by swimming all the way from Florida to Maryland's Chesapeake Bay. That year, after becoming the poster child for manatee conservation up and down the East Coast, the endangered, 10-foot-long, 1,200-pound West Indian manatee got a lift back to Florida aboard an Air Force C-130. Back home, Chessie was equipped with a Telonics satellite–monitored radio tag and released near the Kennedy Space Center on October 7, 1994. That winter he swam to southern Florida.

During the summer of 1995, Chessie again took off from Florida's Merritt Island National Wildlife Refuge to swim all the way to Point Judith, Rhode Island. Covering 20 miles a day, he traveled farther north than any manatee had previously been sighted—the old record being the Potomac River. En route, he stopped along the coast to feed on marsh grass and to ride the surf, typically staying two to three days at a place

"Power plant effluents are occasionally interrupted because of mechanical failure or for scheduled maintenance. During severely cold weather, water temperatures can fall so low (4–8°C.) that even the warmed effluent is too cold for the survival of some manatees."

&

—JANE PACKARD,
Department of Wildlife
and Fisheries,
Texas A&M University

OPPOSITE: *A crinkly skinned calf walks along the bottom of Crystal River as its mother uses her left flipper to scratch her cheek. Due to their smaller size, young manatees are more susceptible to sudden changes in water temperatures.*

before moving on. Biologists with the U.S. Geological Survey were able to track the roving manatee by satellite thanks to radio signals emitted from the floating transmitter attached by a belt to the base of his tail.

It appeared that Chessie had a great trip, visiting Ocean City in Maryland, Atlantic City in New Jersey, the Statue of Liberty, Ellis Island, and Coney Island. In fact, Chessie's travels might explain several old reports of a Loch Ness–type monster spotted in Chesapeake Bay.

Chessie turned south after reaching the cool waters off Rhode Island on August 13, 1995. Soon after, his satellite tag, designed to break free if entangled, detached, and it was recovered off the Connecticut coast on August 22. For the next three months, no one knew where Chessie was, until November 16, when he was spotted once again in the warm waters of Florida.

Sirenia Project biologists succeeded in retagging Chessie in February 1996 while he was wintering in southern Florida, but contact was again lost when his collar released. Late in the summer of 1998, an animal matching Chessie's description was spotted off the tip of Long Island, then again off the coast of New Jersey heading south. Because manatees are such creatures of habit, researchers suspect that this animal was Chessie—once again making his big summertime moves.

"Having documented what an individual of this species can achieve," says Sirenia Project biologist Jim Reid, "it is likely that moves such as Chessie's have been made by other manatees in the past, and that they may be made again in the future."

BELOW: *A trio of manatees floats just beneath the surface at Crystal River. As an adaptation for swimming, manatees have no external earlobes, but they have excellent high-frequency hearing. A tiny ear opening is located just behind each eye.*

"Low reproduction and long
life span are not unique to
manatees, but are part of
the life-history strategies of
some birds, many species of
whales, several herbivores,
and a few carnivores."

⚭

—MIRIAM MARMONTEL,
manatee biologist

LEFT: *This haunting image of
a Florida manatee best captures
their predicament—they are living fossils whose rich evolutionary history predates* Homo
sapiens, *and yet their very survival now depends on us.*

Longevity

Like their distant elephant relatives, sirenians are long lived. They evolved over millions
of years in environments that were relatively stable.

Because manatees continually grow and shed their teeth, another means of aging
them had to be determined. Parts of the manatee's periotic (ear) bones have growth
layers that may persist for the life of the animal. These are used by scientists to estimate a manatee's age during autopsy.

With no natural enemies, Florida manatees can live 60 years or more. For example,
Snooty, the West Indian manatee that resides at the South Florida Museum in
Bradenton, turned 50 in 1998. Scientists estimate that dugongs can live 70 years or
more—under ideal conditions.

But that is the catch-22 for the otherwise long-lived sirenians. Those "ideal conditions" no longer exist in a world overpopulated by *Homo sapiens.*

Manatee Reproduction

MALE AND FEMALE MANATEES LOOK ALIKE, WHICH EXPLAINS why it has been so difficult for scientists to spy on their sex lives. The only way to determine gender is to look at the position of the genital openings (not an easy thing to do), search for a prominent teat under the female's flippered armpit, or look for the swollen dimensions of pregnancy. In other words, there is very little sexual dimorphism in manatees, other than the position of the genital openings—in females, located closest to the tail, just in front of the anus; in males, more toward the center of the belly just below the umbilical scar. The presence of a nursing calf, of course, is usually a good gender clue.

According to Galen Rathbun, a former leader of the federal Sirenia Project based in Gainesville, there are gender differences in behavior. Females have a higher rate of return to winter refuges than males, females with dependent calves arrive at these

LEFT: *A very young manatee calf stays close to his mother's side. Among manatees, the basic social unit and longest-lasting relationship is shared between a mother and her calf. They maintain their close bond through frequent physical contact and "vocal duets" consisting of chirps, squeals, and whistles.*

PRECEDING PAGE: *A mother and calf. The prolonged dependency of manatee calves on their mothers is adaptive. It takes time to learn the migration routes to feeding sites and critical warm-water refuges in which to pass the cold winter months.*

sites in advance of most males, and females with calves are less prone than other females and males to wander far from warm-water refuges between winter cold spells.

"The age at which individuals begin reproducing is an important point in the life history," says University of Florida biologist Miriam Marmontel. "Age at sexual maturation, age at first parturition, and age-specific fecundity are valuable biological parameters for population modeling and, coupled with mortality, influence the ability of a population to replace itself."

Such information is particularly important for an endangered species such as the manatee.

"Dozens of wild females have now been observed for more than a decade—some of them for nearly three—giving us insight into their reproductive cycle," says former Sirenia Project leader Thomas O'Shea. "A female attains sexual maturity as young as three years of age and continues to reproduce for more than 20 years. One calf is born every 2½ to 5 years; there are occasionally even twins."

M a n a t e e   R e p r o d u c t i o n

Mating Herds

Manatees noticeably pick up their bucolic pace during the spring and early-summer months, when mating and calving activity peaks. Forever on the lookout for receptive females, manatee males often travel great distances in their search. It is an adaptive reproductive strategy, as mature females seem to have an estrous cycle that approximates a lunar month. The females are polyestrous (have more than one estrous cycle per year) and will continue to cycle until they become pregnant.

Among terrestrial ungulates, the males of many species test a female's readiness to mate by sniffing and tasting her urine. Ed Gerstein, director of marine mammal research at Florida Atlantic University, has found that manatees can detect different salinity gradients in the water, and suggests that male manatees may also use chemoreceptive abilities to detect estrous females—by "tasting" their reproductive pheromones in the water.

This would help to explain how a fertile female manatee manages to attract 5 to 22 unrelated but eager males who are willing to escort her closely for up to a month. Males appear to establish a rank order for copulation access, and females may choose particular males with which to mate. Pursued by a horde of jostling, wrestling males, the female becomes the focal point of the "estrous herd." In an attempt to evade her persistent suitors, the female will often twist and turn violently.

"Perhaps the greatest flaw in what is otherwise a design for an idyllic life is in the sex lives of manatees," wrote author Faith McNulty. "Male manatees are very sexy and female manatees are not. As a cow comes into estrus, there is a long period during which she is intensely attractive to males but is quite uninclined to mate. Consequently, she collects a train of increasingly frantic suitors, who pester her relentlessly."

According to pioneering manatee biologist Daniel Hartman, this arrangement encourages selective competition among the males for the privilege of mating. It is during the formation of these mating herds that the manatees go from docile to pushy as the males vie for water space near the female, bouncing and bumping one another, even crawling over each other's backs with their flippers.

"Younger males may come and go, but a nucleus of mature bulls is always present to escort the cow wherever she leads them," wrote Hartman *(National Geographic,* September 1969). "One day a cow and her train filed past me as if in review. There were 17 escorts in her retinue—nearly the entire male constituency of Crystal River!"

At Blue Lagoon, John Reynolds watched estrous females swim into shoals to prevent the males from reaching their undersides to mate. Once in shallow water, the resistant female would raise her tail and swat the approaching males. Because the males do not defend territories around the female, they put all of their energy into remaining near her.

The pursuing males are mild tempered, though persistent, colliding with each other in play and occasional mock-sexual behavior rather than aggression. If they show any aggression at all, it is subtle, consisting of pushing, shoving, bumping, and piling up on

LEFT: *Only when a female is in estrus and a group of eligible males herd around her, do manatees appear most active. The males gently push and bump into one another as they attempt to gain access to the female.*

BELOW: *While pursued by a mating herd of persistent males, a female may mate with several bulls before going off to give birth and raise the calf by herself.*

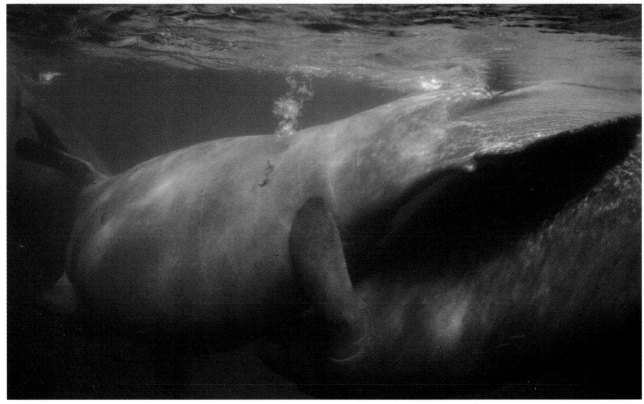

IN THE COMPANY OF MANATEES

one another in an effort to gain access to the female. This type of herd formation usually lasts the length of time a female is sexually receptive. During this time, mating appears to be random, the cow mating with several different bulls.

Copulation takes place at the surface and underwater in a variety of positions: both male and female horizontal, vertical, on their sides facing each other, and sometimes with the bull turned upside down swimming below the cow.

According to Hartman, not all aggregations of manatees that engage in mating behaviors are heterosexual. In the warm-water refugia of Florida, all-male groups may cavort intensely for several hours at a time. It has been proposed that such all-male gatherings may represent contests of stamina in which males practice behavior patterns used in mating while possibly establishing some sort of rank or hierarchy.

Manatees do not form permanent pair bonds. The male's only reproductive role occurs during courtship as a participant in a transitory mating herd. As the female's receptive period ends, the males disperse, leaving the female, if pregnant, to care for the calf herself. The relationship that eventually forms between a mother and her calf is the only long-term stable bond found in manatees.

Birth

Following a gestation period of 385 to 400 days, females usually seek quiet backwater areas to give birth. Arriving tail first, a 60- to 70-pound calf (about the size of a weaner pig) is born, measuring about 4 feet in length. The newborn swims to the surface for its first breath of air, and begins to vocalize soon after birth.

There are reports in the literature that female manatees help support their calves at the surface until they get used to breathing on their own. However, they do not hug their calves with their flippers while they nurse, as has also been reported. In fact, the only time Blue Spring State Park ranger Wayne Hartley has seen a female manatee put her flippers around her calf was when a mother manatee named Julie did so to protect her calf Jollymon from the advances of a male known as Crazy Nick.

Usually a single calf is produced, but twins do occur. During her study of manatee carcasses in Florida, Miriam Marmontel at the University of Florida found that roughly 4 percent of the pregnant females in her sample were carrying twin fetuses. This figure corresponds to the twinning rate reported for African elephants, but it was higher than the percentage of twins actually observed in the wild among a larger sample of nursing manatee young.

Data collected during aerial surveys, carcass salvage, and necropsy of pregnant females indicate that most Florida manatee calves are born in spring and early summer. Marmontel believes that a spring breeding and birthing season may offer advantages to both female manatees and their young. Milder spring and summer temperatures probably help reduce the energetic stress on lactating females and newborn calves, resulting in greater survival rates for the calves. This corresponds with the synchronized calving seasons shared by other large herbivores such as the wildebeest, gazelle, and zebra,

OPPOSITE, TOP LEFT: *Manatees are promiscuous; they do not mate for life. Instead, males form temporary mating herds around a receptive female.*

OPPOSITE, TOP RIGHT: *Females often take evasive action with body twists and tail slaps to thwart the unwanted attention of amorous males until the female is ready to mate.*

OPPOSITE, BELOW: *A combination of male rank and female choice ultimately determines which animals will mate.*

"In some cases, the flanks of pregnant females visibly undulate as a result of fetal movements."

—GALEN RATHBUN, *former project leader, USGS Sirenia Project*

which give birth at the start of the rainy season, when plant growth best supports lactating females and their young.

Lactation

Soon after birth, the calf begins to nurse underwater from one of its mother's two mammary glands, which are located beneath her flippers. Manatee milk contains more fats, proteins, and salt than cow's milk, but it does not contain lactose. As the calf gets more proficient, nursing frequency and duration increase.

To watch a calf nurse is both endearing and comical. The crinkly-skinned calf appears to glomp securely onto its mother's armpit just behind her flipper with its strong lips. This is the way the calf will continue to nurse for the next 18 months or more, even as it begins to approach the size of its mother.

Mother and calf stay together as a nursing pair for at least a year, usually longer.

ABOVE: *Manatee calves have an endearing relationship with their devoted mothers. Here a calf rests on its mother's back at Blue Spring State Park.*

RIGHT: *Manatee calves can be real hams, as this one is, resting upside down in the shallow water next to its mother. (Photo courtesy the Florida Department of Environmental Protection)*

The pair maintains contact while they swim and feed with vocalizations that have been described as squeaking, whistling duets. The calves move in synchrony with their mothers, surfacing to breathe when she does and dozing on the bottom in close contact. Should the mother sense danger, she will place herself between her calf and the perceived threat.

"One predictable vocal reaction is the alarm duet between a mother and her calf as she calls it to her side before fleeing," says Hartman, ". . . when frightened a manatee may light out at speeds close to twenty miles an hour, churning the water to a froth."

Manatee calves begin to nibble at plant material a few weeks after birth, yet most calves remain with their mothers for close to two years or more. The prolonged nursing relationship helps to maintain the close mother-infant bond, but it probably becomes more affiliative than nutritional as the calf approaches weaning. Research suggests that mothers and their young recognize each other beyond weaning and that some offspring spend at least their subadult lives within the range of their mother.

At Blue Spring, Wayne Hartley has seen weaned calves return to hang out with their mother and younger half sib, and females adopt weaned calves when they have lost their own new calves. He has also watched manatee calves sneak nursing bouts from females not related to them. "Some mothers will nurse any calf that comes up and asks," says Hartley. "Then there are other moms that say 'No way.'"

ABOVE: *A playful manatee calf embraces his mother's head with his flippers.*

"The most complex manatee behavior is between mother and calf."

☙☙

—AKEMI HOTTA, *in* Manatee

IN THE COMPANY OF MANATEES

OPPOSITE: *Because male and female manatees look alike, it is difficult to tell them apart. The presence of mammary glands under the flippers reveals that this animal is a female.*

LEFT: *Although they begin to eat plants a few weeks after birth, manatee calves often nurse for up to two years or more as part of the close nurturing bond between mother and calf.*

BELOW: *Manatee calves begin nursing underwater soon after birth. Because the mother's teats are located beneath the folds of her flippers, it often looks like the calf is sucking on her armpit.*

Birth Interval

OPPOSITE: *Some manatee mothers don't mind if a calf other than their own sneaks a suckle now and then. Females that lose their calves frequently adopt orphaned or newly weaned calves.*

Among Florida manatees, the birth interval between calves can range from 2½ to 5 years, depending on the age of the previous calf at weaning, the age and health of the female, the duration of any post-weaning recovery period, missed opportunities for conception, failed pregnancies, and dependent calf mortalities. Scientists have calculated that under very optimum conditions, a healthy female manatee might be able to produce 12 to 14 young in her lifetime.

Juliet, a female manatee brought to the Miami Seaquarium in 1958, was still reproducing after 35 years in captivity. A 29-year-old female designated M-331 was carrying twins when she died after a boat collision in 1983. Thirty-five-year-old KDL-8867 had just given birth a few weeks before her carcass was found, and pushing 39 years of age, KDL-8745 had recently given birth and was lactating when she drowned in a shrimper's net.

A slow, low reproductive rate, spread out over a long life span, is a pattern seen in many other mammalian species, including primates, whales, elephants, rhinos, and the large carnivores. Such a reproductive strategy is possible only in a very stable environment, with well-established, nearly permanent geographic ranges, and among species that are relatively free from serious predation. This explains why humans have had such a devastating impact on the planet's slow-reproducing species. Evolving over millions of years in relatively stable environments, they were not designed to survive overhunting, habitat loss, and fierce competition for resources with *Homo sapiens*.

Calf Mortality

According to Bruce Ackerman of the Florida Department of Environmental Protection, the number of very young calves that die each year has been increasing. Speculative, yet unproven, reasons offered include pollution, disease, unsuccessful first attempts at birth or nursing by increasing numbers of younger females, and the orphaning of young due to maternal disturbance or mortality.

Daniel Hartman described the intense and "unrelenting pursuit" of females by herds of "bulls," including "violent jack-knife[s]" and "frenzied embraces," and also noted that these pursuits are sometimes of females with calves. Wayne Hartley and Tom O'Shea documented the birth of a calf in the quiet backwater of Ziegler Dead River near Blue Spring. Five days later the female was pursued by a lone male who persistently "pushed and thrashed her" as she and her newborn calf moved slowly through the shallow water. Following within a few feet, the male repeatedly contacted and attempted to mount the female. She responded with lunges above the water surface, apparently trying to get away. Both O'Shea and Hartley speculate that such male behavior may result in calf mortality.

"One may envision young calves being left behind or lost as females try to elude pursuing males," explains O'Shea, "calves that are stressed from trying to keep up with their mothers and having their nursing patterns interrupted, or calves that are physically

injured or drowned during the intense pursuits of females by males. Calves may also die if males interrupt females during parturition."

Scientists have described the movement patterns of male manatees during the spring and summer months in the St. Johns River as "patrolling circuits" in search of estrous females. Male manatees on the Gulf Coast also show greater rates and wider ranges of travel. Possibly as a response to the roving males, late-term pregnant females swim a few miles away from their normal home range to give birth in quiet canals, boat basins, and secluded backwater areas far away from the main channels of male travel.

According to O'Shea, male mating strategies involving infanticide are known for a variety of mammals. Loss of newborn manatee calves would be advantageous to male manatees if females became estrous soon after the death of their calves. In fact, manatee females have been observed in estrus just 10 to 15 days after the loss of a calf at birth.

O'Shea points out that manatees of weaning age and size are most susceptible to mortality in winter. To compensate, manatee mothers tend to suppress weaning behavior from November to February, supplying their calves instead with energy-rich milk and guidance to winter food sources and warm-water retreats. However, the death rate of even younger calves (between late pregnancy and first winter) is highest of all, and has ranged from 33 percent at Crystal River to 40 percent at Blue Spring.

RIGHT: *A calf's crinkled skin, which develops over time due to a fungus reaction, is seen most often among Crystal River manatees.*

Mother as Teacher

The quarter-century study of manatees at Blue Spring State Park has revealed a great deal of variation in the quality and duration of maternal care. According to biologist Tom O'Shea, some females wean calves at 14 to 15 months; others retain nursing calves until they are two years of age or older. However, two things have been consistent for all mothers: birth and weaning do not tend to occur during the winter months.

Most significant, independent calves continue to inhabit their mother's home range long after weaning. Manatees mix and travel together during the summer, at which time older offspring often meet and tag along with their mothers. Such prolonged contact facilitates the transmission of traditional information from mother to offspring, including the location of warm-water refuges, feeding sites, and preferred travel routes.

That this information is critical to survival is illustrated by the fact that a large number of the manatees that succumb to extremely cold weather each winter are the size of animals experiencing their first winter on their own. Young manatees appear to need a long tutorial period with their mothers in order to learn the seasonal migration routes to and from warm-water habitats and the location of the best food sources needed to survive. This finding alone has important implications for proposed conservation strategies to breed manatees in captivity and release them into the wild. Without prolonged lessons in the wild from a manatee mom, young captive-bred manatees have an even greater risk of mortality when released to open waters.

"Survival over a long life span both requires and facilitates the acquisition of considerable experience," explained zoologist Richard F. Barnes of Rwanda's Karisoke Research Centre. His observations were made on African elephants, which, like their sirenian relatives, have a prolonged period of juvenile dependency. "By continuing to guide her family unit long after she is too old to breed, the matriarch can enhance the

LEFT: *Following a 12- to 13-month gestation period, a single calf is born—rarely twins. At birth, a calf weighs 60 to 65 pounds and measures about 4 feet in length.*

IN THE COMPANY OF MANATEES

survival of her offspring by providing them with the benefits of her accumulated experience: her knowledge of their home range, of seasonal water sources and ephemeral food supplies, and of sources of danger and ways of avoiding them."

Adoption

Female manatees appear to have big hearts. They readily adopt orphaned calves, both in the wild and in captivity, as well as calves that have been weaned but return to beg for extended maternal care. Take, for example, a one-year-old calf named Gummi Bear at Blue Spring State Park. He begged for adoption by floating on his back in front of Lily, a seasoned manatee mother but not his own, and hit his mouth repeatedly with his flippers to make a funny splashing noise—until Lily agreed to adopt him. She then treated him like her own calf, protecting him from people.

Over the years, numerous incidents at the Miami Seaquarium have demonstrated just how nurturing female manatees can be. When a baby manatee with severe lacerations was rescued near Port Everglades after being hit by a boat, the injured and orphaned baby was behaviorally adopted by a four-year-old female at the aquarium who had never even been a mother. Naples, a female manatee at the Miami Seaquarium, gave birth to her own calf, Harvey, while simultaneously adopting a three-week-old orphaned calf named Timehri. She nursed them both.

OPPOSITE: *Two calves appear to dance as they play together at Crystal River.*

ABOVE: *Dappled sunlight plays across the backs of a mother and calf at Blue Spring State Park. At birth, calves weigh but a fraction of their mothers' total body weight.*

Manatees in Jeopardy

THE MANATEE'S SLOW-MOTION LIFE IN LILY-PAD PASTURES
sounds idyllic—and would be, if not for the intrusion of humans. Since 1994, 200 or
more manatees have died each year in U.S. waters. In 1996 these numbers doubled
when a red tide killed 12 percent of Florida's entire west-coast population. During an
average year at least a third of all manatee deaths are caused by humans—a quarter
from collision with boats or barges. Powerboat propellers can repeatedly slice the back
of a manatee in seconds, sending the wounded animal to the bottom to drown or eventually die of septicemia (blood poisoning).

It is estimated that more than 80 percent of Florida's 2,000-plus manatees are
propeller-scarred. Most adults carry an assortment of marks from multiple injuries.
Ironically, most of what is now known about manatee biology is the result of long-
term recognition of individual animals made possible by the scars and deformities

PRECEDING PAGE:
Manatees compete with people for water space in Florida where boats outnumber manatees 500 to 1.

ABOVE: *Florida's Crystal River is an important stronghold for manatees on the Gulf Coast. In 1997, a 94-foot, 150-passenger cruise ship began running gambling tours up and down the shallow river, until arrests and lawsuits shut down the operation.*

caused by encounters with boats (and entanglement in fishing gear). Yet propellers aren't the only danger to manatees. Roughly 50 percent of the animals killed by "boat hits" are killed upon impact with the hull and not by injury from the propeller.

According to Save the Manatee Club, manatee deaths caused by large boats generally fall into one of two categories: the manatee is crushed against the bottom of the waterway by a barge, or it is "sucked into" the large propeller of a tugboat or ship. When crushing occurs, the internal injuries seen are "bilateral," meaning they are present on both sides of the manatee's body. In turn, large propellers cause very large cuts, sometimes completely severing the body in one or more places. Field data now indicate that the vast majority of injuries seen in manatees result from encounters with boats in the "recreational" size class. Both inboard and outboard motors can kill or injure manatees.

The following terse report filed by a researcher at the Sirenia Project's Gainesville lab best illustrates the gruesome deaths suffered by these gentle mammals: "Sex of specimen: female. Length: 8.4 feet. Cause of death: six broken ribs, right side, punctured lung, diaphragm torn from cavity wall. Boat/barge collision."

In addition, manatees are often drowned and crushed in floodgates and caught in sewer pipes. Dependent manatee calves are occasionally separated from their mothers by man-made constructions. Fishing hooks can become embedded in the animals' lips and intestines, and monofilament from fishing lines and crab traps often wraps so tightly around their flippers that it results in blood poisoning or the loss of a limb.

"The bottom line," says Judith Vallee, executive director of Save the Manatee Club, "is Florida's waterways are unsafe."

Why Endangered

The Sirenia appeared more than 50 million years ago during the Eocene Era. Different species and genera have come and gone since then. The four species that survive are considered relic species from this ancient lineage. Their long evolutionary history puts them closer in time to the dinosaurs than to humans. In fact, their association with people has been but a recent blip on an otherwise long, uneventful timeline. For millions of years, the Sirenia evolved in plant-munching peace—until *Homo sapiens* arrived on the scene.

Zero Population Growth, based in Washington, D.C., offers some illustrative statistics as to why animals such as the endangered manatees and dugongs are feeling the squeeze: When Columbus sailed to the New World in 1492, the world population stood at about 500 million. When Thomas Jefferson became the third president of the United States in 1801, it had reached 1 billion. It took another century to reach 2 billion, with succeeding increments of 1 billion taking 33 years, 14 years, and 13 years. The next billion people will be added in just 11 years.

The U.S. Census Bureau projects that in the year 2000, the population of the United States will exceed 275 million, more than double the 1940 population. By 2050, the nation's population is projected to increase by nearly 130 million people—the equivalent of adding another four states the size of California. Such rapid growth has caused severe environmental repercussions. According to the World Resources Institute, in the last 200 years, the United States has lost 50 percent of its wetlands, 90 percent of its northwestern old-growth forests, and 99 percent of its tall grass prairie. Every day an estimated 9 square miles of rural land in the United States is lost to development.

Of even more significance to the Sirenia, the condition of the ocean environment is now declining at an unprecedented rate. To call attention to the rapid loss of ocean resources, biodiversity, and maritime coastal economies, 1998 was declared the International Year of the Ocean by UNESCO and the UN General Assembly, who believe that neither governments nor the public have paid adequate attention to the need to protect the marine environment to ensure a healthy ocean.

According to a report issued by IUCN–World Conservation Union's Magnus Ngoile in 1997, "the earth's oceans and seas cover 71 percent of the planet and contain much of the earth's biological diversity in its many biomes. Therefore the oceans and coasts are important for the existence of life on earth, providing resources and services to human society. Approximately 75–80 percent of world trade (six trillion dollars annually) and 60 percent of the tourism industry (three trillion dollars annually) is ocean dependent. More than 50 percent of the world population currently resides in a coastal strip extending 60 km [37 miles] from the shoreline. By the year 2020, it is estimated that the coastal population will be 75 percent of the total."

"We are in a race. Maybe we should call it a contest. A lot of the things that are happening, like the threats to biodiversity, are the products of rather innocent actions. Population growth is the result of reproductive patterns that were an integral part of our survival as a species. It has now become a real threat."

～

—LESTER R. BROWN,
President,
Worldwatch Institute

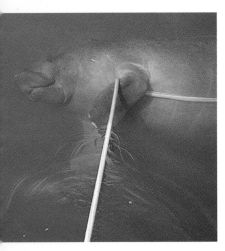

ABOVE: *Manatees often use their flippers to playfully grasp anchor lines. Unfortunately, this playful behavior often leads to entanglement and injuries.*

"I wonder about this Florida sometimes. One has to look harder for nature nowadays. I sometimes find it neatly woven into the tapestry of a park or a preserve.... Increasingly, this natural Florida greets me right smack in the middle of urbanization. The effect is both comforting and oddly jarring, like hearing a Bach requiem in the food court of a garish shopping mall."

—BILL BELLEVILLE, in *Sierra,* October 1977

Florida represents a microcosm of this global dilemma. The Sunshine State is now the fourth-fastest-growing state in the United States, with a population of 14.7 million people in 1997—75 percent of whom live along the state's already crowded coasts. In addition to the nearly 560 people a day who move to the state, more than 47 million people visit there each year. Florida continues to be the number one tourist destination in the United States: more than 80 percent of Orlando's tourists return within three to five years. Eighty-nine Fortune 500 companies have a presence in the Metro Orlando area. In 1995, if you wanted to stay in all of the guest rooms then available on Disney's Orlando properties, it would have taken 61 years—staying in one room a night.

Such a relentless human invasion has put the slow-speed manatees on an environmental collision course with man. Gone are many of the freshwater and marine grassbeds they once depended on—as the result of water pollution, herbicides, surface runoff, and dredge and fill projects. An estimated 80 percent of Florida's seagrass beds have been destroyed since 1960. According to a report published by Defenders of Wildlife in 1995, Florida's ecosystems are more at risk than those of any other state in the United States because of rapid, ongoing development.

"What most people don't realize is that the dredged canals, landfill, and seawalls required to develop wetlands can severely alter drainage patterns, nutrient exchange, and filtering functions, all of which are necessary to maintain the abundant food supply and clean, unpolluted water vital to manatees," explains Texas A&M University biologist Jane Packard, who compared a variety of survey techniques in the 1980s to assess manatee population size.

Mortality Statistics

"According to population theory," wrote *Nature Conservancy* editor William Stolzenburg, "the fewer the individuals, the more potentially devastating the purely random forces of nature. A roll of the demographic dice can leave a small population with too many old, too few females, too little genetic variability—too little internal rebound to survive. Natural catastrophes, like fires, storms, droughts and disease—blows that might dent a big population—can crush a small one."

This explains why scientists watch the annual mortality numbers for Florida manatees so carefully. It wouldn't take much by way of disease or natural disaster to reduce their already endangered population to the point of no recovery. And the trend doesn't look promising. In 1996, 2,639 manatees were counted during statewide aerial surveys. Just two years later, the number had dropped to 2,019.

During the winter of 1989–1990, many manatees died from cold stress as the result of a prolonged cold front in December that caused Florida's coastal water temperatures to drop into the 40° to 50°F. range. "Cold snaps, dangerous to all manatees, are particularly deadly to the young," says Loren Fish, supervisor of animal care at SeaWorld Orlando. "When the water gets below 68 degrees, the young can't tolerate it. They develop pneumonia and stop eating. Unusually cold weather killed 53 manatees in 1990."

The following mortality statistics are provided by the Florida Department of Environmental Protection, Florida Marine Research Institute for the United States and Puerto Rico. As indicated, some years were better than others for manatees. However, since 1993, the overall trend has been for an ever increasing number of dead manatees.

YEAR	NUMBER DEAD	YEAR	NUMBER DEAD
1979	78	1989	176
1980	65	1990	214
1981	117	1991	175
1982	117	1992	167
1983	81	1993	147
1984	130	1994	195
1985	123	1995	203
1986	125	1996	416
1987	117	1997	242
1988	134	1998	231

Although these statistics vary by year, the determined cause of most manatee deaths falls statistically into the following categories:

Unknown (manatee too decomposed to determine)	32%
Watercraft collisions	23%
Dependent calf (less than 60 inches in length)	21%
Other natural causes (stress, cold, red tide, disease)	17%
Floodgates/canal locks	4%
Other human	3%

Boats and Barges

As humorist Dave Barry once wrote, things were going pretty well for manatees until the earth's climate changed, allowing the emergence of one of the most dangerous forces in all of nature: the recreational motorboater. "I used to do some recreational motorboating," he said, "and I can tell you for a fact that there are recreational boaters out there whose nautical alertness is such that they would not immediately notice if they drove their boats into a shopping center food court."

Florida's 2,000 or so manatees compete with more than 1 million boaters vying for the same water space. In 1998, of the 809,160 registered boats in the state, 769,527 of them were coastal pleasure craft. These are joined each year by an estimated 300,000 to 400,000 out-of-state boaters, who add to the aquatic frey. These statistics explain why Florida leads the nation in the number of human fatalities from boating accidents each

"Some people in Florida are openly antagonistic toward regulations that restrict human activities. The attitude has been publicly expressed: waterways belong to humans and, if manatees and other creatures cannot exist where people want to boat or ski, that is unfortunate."

—JOHN E. REYNOLDS, *chairman, U.S. Marine Mammal Commission*

"It's a question of politics and money. Boating is big business in Florida. It is a conflict here—manatees versus growth and business.."

—DANIEL ODELL, *veterinarian, SeaWorld Orlando*

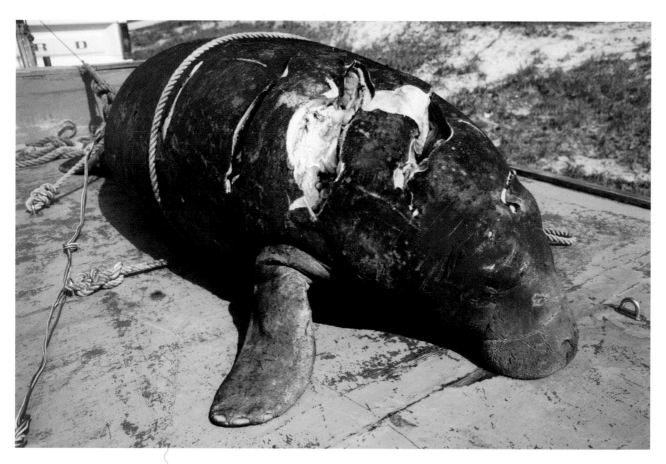

ABOVE: *A manatee dies from boat wounds in Hobe Sound. Propeller wounds become fatal when they cut into the body cavity. (Photo courtesy of the USGS Sirenia Project)*

RIGHT: *Deaths caused by watercraft collisions are one of the few preventable causes of death faced by manatees. (Photo courtesy of the Florida Department of Environmental Protection/Tom Pitchford)*

year. They are also foreboding numbers for Florida's endangered manatees, with boats outnumbering manatees 500 to 1.

"With all of these boats," says Save the Manatee Club's executive director, Judith Vallee, "there are only 400 law enforcement officers patrolling the state's waterways. The Florida Marine Patrol is stretched way too thin, and without an adequate enforcement presence, voluntary compliance with manatee boat-speed regulations is probably low."

In 1995, Mote Marine Laboratory senior biologist Jay Gorzelany worked with the Florida Department of Environmental Protection to study boater compliance in conjunction with speed-zone regulations in Sarasota County. More than 32,000 vessels were observed and evaluated by air-, boat-, and land-based surveys. A laser-targeted speed gun was also used to evaluate boat speeds in the 25-mph restricted portions of the Intercoastal Waterway. While approximately 60 percent of boaters in Sarasota County were found to be in compliance with posted speed regulations, specific recreational-watersports areas had only 50 percent compliance, and personal watercraft (i.e., jet skis) showed the least compliance of all vessel types, averaging only 36 percent.

Because manatees prefer shallow water, surface to breathe air, swim slowly, and like to doze and float just beneath the surface, they are extremely vulnerable to "boat hits." The slow-going, half-ton or larger mammals usually do not have time to maneuver out of the path of an oncoming speedboat, and their preferred shallow-water habitat doesn't leave them much room to dive deeper.

Identifying a boat's location and path of travel is hard to do underwater, even for human divers, because the engine sounds seem to come from all directions at once. In fact, after more than 3,000 hours of study, Lowry Park Zoo biologist Edmund Gerstein and his wife, Laura, concluded that boat noises do not fall within the manatees' optimum hearing range. They found that even in still, quiet water, the animals can't hear a boat until the craft is right on top of them.

This means that Florida manatees are on the losing side of an escalating invasion of their shallow-water habitats. Boat fatalities, it turns out, are the leading cause of known fatalities for this endangered species. As a result, various ideas have been proposed to give the manatees a fighting chance, including mandatory installation of propeller guards on all powerboats, equipping boats with underwater alarms, and the passage of a statewide boating speed limit that would encourage the fastest boats to move out of the inland waterways and into the Gulf and open ocean.

In the meantime, residents living along the beautiful Myakka River in Sarasota County approached county commissioners in 1997 to oppose the slow boat speeds posted on the Myakka, Florida's only nationally recognized "wild and scenic river." The disgruntled homeowners claimed that it took them too long to get down the narrow, winding river—a river frequented by canoeists, kayakers, and manatees.

"Without public cooperation and support," says Lynn Lefebvre, director of the Sirenia Project, "the seemingly unavoidable increase in Florida's human population and numbers of boaters will crush any hope of achieving a sustainable manatee population in Florida."

"It is easy to identify a manatee. All you have to do is look for the big, white propeller scars on its back or the chunks missing from its paddle-shaped tail. Nearly every adult manatee comes with its own unique set of hatch marks, often from multiple collisions. And they are the lucky ones: they survived."

〜

—JAY GORZELANY,
Senior Biologist,
Mote Marine Laboratory

"People who care about manatees need to get on the phone and let their legislators know how they feel while there's still time," adds Judith Vallee. "Without adequate boating education and regulations that are well enforced, manatees are doomed."

Harassment

Well-meaning people often unknowingly cause the most harm to manatees. Few realize that it is illegal to touch a manatee, let alone chase one out of its warm-water habitat. Harassment by divers, boaters, swimmers, and those casting fishing lines can force manatees to abandon their preferred warm-water habitats. Whether intentional or negligent, harassment can also separate mothers from their calves.

"Anything that disrupts the manatees' normal behavior is considered harassment," explains Pat Rose, director of government relations with Save the Manatee Club. This can include chasing, poking, grabbing, prodding, riding, and feeding them, or giving them water from a hose. When conditioned to take food or water from people, the trusting animals become more vulnerable to malicious individuals who might try to feed them dangerous nonfood items or harm them in some other way.

As a result, Save the Manatee Club supports only passive observation. "The only way to interact with manatees and other wildlife," says Rose, "is to view them from a distance."

"When the public finds manatees, it often hassles them or, worse, 'helps' them by feeding them such foods as pizza, which you rarely find growing naturally in the underwater environment."

ᛣᚱ

—DAVE BARRY

Infatuated Divers

Crystal River lures a great number of people to its spring-fed waters each year because it is the only place in Florida (and the world) where the public can legally don snorkeling gear to swim with manatees.

Between 100 and 125 commercial fishing boats and guides operate out of Crystal River. On a typical winter weekend, as many as 600 to 800 divers rent snorkeling and scuba equipment to swim with the mammals. Although seven areas are off-limits to boats and divers, it is not uncommon to see divers inside sanctuary boundaries as manatees swim outside. Overenthusiastic divers can force the animals away from their warmwater refuges during wintertime, when temperature regulation is most critical for the manatees.

"Reports of people riding, chasing, and actually sitting and standing on manatees are not uncommon," says Save the Manatee Club executive director Judith Vallee. "This is alarming, considering an estimated 80,000 to 100,000 divers visit Crystal River annually."

A Culture of Violence

Envision any high-speed recreational boat—from jet skis and ski boats to roaring cigarette-hull speedboats—and the person behind the wheel is usually male. Registered

BELOW: *A manatee patiently waits to have her injured flipper medicated at Tampa's Lowry Park Zoo after getting it entangled with a rope. (Photo courtesy Lowry Park Zoo)*

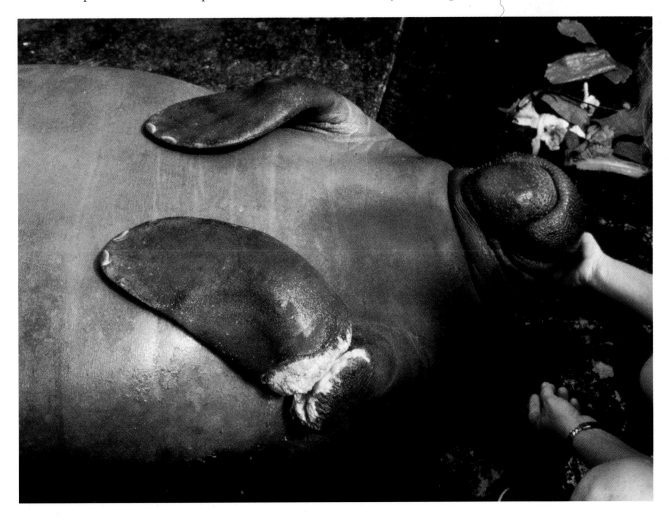

boat owners are also more likely to be male. Given the fact that men tend to be more authority resistant and greater risk takers than women, then boating, with ever faster hull designs and more powerful engines, is an ideal environment for the expression of such tendencies. Add alcohol or drugs to the macho, speed- and thrill-seeking equation, and it's easy to see why so many people lose their lives on Florida's waterways each year—not to mention manatees.

According to Scott Wright and Bruce Ackerman of the Florida Department of Environmental Protection, Florida Marine Research Institute, witnessed collisions between manatees and watercraft are rarely reported to authorities. Of nearly 600 documented watercraft-related manatee deaths recorded up to 1995, details such as boat size, speed, or engine horsepower were known for only about 20 of them.

"Because so few strikes occurred to the head and most strikes occurred over the kidneys and tail, the animals may have been diving when struck," say Wright and Ackerman. "We cannot determine the direction into which the boat was traveling from the scar pattern . . . in 89 percent of the strikes we documented, the animal was either facing or moving directly away from the oncoming boat when struck . . . nearly 90 percent of the scar patterns were along the head-to-tail axis, indicating manatees were moving *in response* to an oncoming boat when struck."

Having witnessed boaters trying to run down Canada geese and other waterfowl, illegally empty bilge tanks into waterways, overfill gas tanks to create surface oil slicks, and break posted speed limits—I'd have to say this leaves room for speculation that not all manatee deaths due to "boat hits" are accidental.

When a herd of manatees made an unusual visit to Shell Island, near Panama City, Florida, in June 1997, they passed by members of the Panama City Dive Club who were picnicking with their families on the island. As the manatees swam by in water only 3 to 4 feet deep, club members splashed into the water to get a closer look.

"The kids were pretty good," said photographer Shirley Brown, "but there was one yahoo with a waverunner chasing the animals around. I could tell they were stressed. They breathed faster and came to the surface more often to breathe. They also moved faster, and manatees aren't very fast animals."

Despite this, Wayne Hartley and other manatee biologists continue to give most boaters the benefit of the doubt. "You can damage your boat pretty good when you hit a manatee," says Hartley. "One researcher watched a boater speed over a manatee, and the impact threw his engine clear out of the water. The guy never saw the manatee and thought he had hit a log."

Human Cruelty

Blue Spring State Park was established in 1972. Prior to that, unsupervised swimmers used the spring run as a party spot, chasing, roping, and riding the wintering manatees. Rangers first assigned to the newly formed park discovered manatees with old ropes tied around them, and others that had been stabbed and beaten.

"No humane being, past the thoughtless age of boyhood, will wantonly murder another creature which holds its life by the same tenure as he does."

֎

—HENRY DAVID THOREAU

"It is a sad but true fact: because of the manatee's size and strange looks, some people have felt compelled to spear them with pitchforks, blast them with shotguns, attack them with axes, carve their initials in them, or deliberately run them down with speedboats."

֎

—M. TIMOTHY O'KEEFE
in Manatees: Our
Vanishing Mermaids

While such unfathomable acts of cruelty are less common than they used to be, manatees still suffer needlessly at the hands of careless, as well as sadistic, people.

In 1990 a Jacksonville fisherman discovered the mutilated carcass of a large male manatee tied to a bridge post along Little Pottsburg Creek. Numerous deep wounds covered its stomach, sides, and back. The Florida Department of Natural Resources (DNR; now the Florida Department of Environmental Protection) was notified, but by the time DNR officers arrived at the scene a few hours later, the carcass had disappeared. It eventually showed up floating 7 miles *upstream* in the Trout River, from all appearances the victim of a boat hit. However, an autopsy revealed that the dead manatee had suffered an extremely violent death—not by boat propeller, but at the hands of a particularly cruel person. The manatee had been gaff-hooked in the head and stabbed 27 times with a knife.

In the fall of 1997, animal rights activists posted a $10,000 reward to catch the killer of a 13-foot, 2,200-pound female manatee that washed up on the shores of Eau Gallie Harbor near Melbourne, Florida, with seven gashes that had pierced her body cavity and punctured her lungs.

"We really believe it's just an outrageous incident," said Save the Manatee Club spokesperson Nancy Sadusky at the time. "We don't think an act of this nature should go unpunished." An unidentified Melbourne businessman matched the $5,000 reward offered by Save the Manatee Club. Despite this, the person who committed the crime was never found.

What a sad statement about human nature that we belittle that which we do not understand, harass those perceived as different from us, and readily exploit the gentle (gullible), weak (vulnerable), and less intelligent. Worst of all are the individuals who get a kick out of intentionally inflicting physical pain on anyone else—be it a person, a pet, or a docile creature such as the manatee.

"Manatees are sort of the perfect victim," concludes Pat Rose of Save the Manatee Club, "because they can't defend themselves and they are not capable of any kind of aggression."

Fishing Conflicts

As the only plant-eating marine mammals in existence today, the Sirenia have little competition for food. Yet since the arrival of *Homo sapiens,* they have had tremendous competition for habitat. Not only have most of their historic seagrass grazing areas been destroyed, but those that remain now attract an armada of people armed with fishing poles, nets, and the latest hook, line, and sinkers.

In fact, fishing is one of the most popular outdoor activities in Florida, and the best place to drop a line is right in the middle of prime manatee habitat—their remaining grazing areas. Rich in marine life, the estuaries and coastal seagrass beds are some of the most productive areas to fish.

The warm-water discharge areas around hydroelectric power plants attract not only

"I am pessimistic about the human race because it is too ingenious for its own good. Our approach to nature is to beat it into submission. We would stand a better chance of survival if we accommodated ourselves to this planet and viewed it appreciatively instead of skeptically and dictatorially."

— E. B. White

"I consider that manatee recovery and protection are, in fact, in jeopardy for four fundamental reasons:

(1) the poorly managed human population growth in Florida,

(2) insufficient funds for acquisition of habitat and enforcement of regulations,

(3) the increasing strength and effectiveness of opposition, and

(4) the size of the problem."

—John E. Reynolds, *chairman, U.S. Marine Mammal Commission*

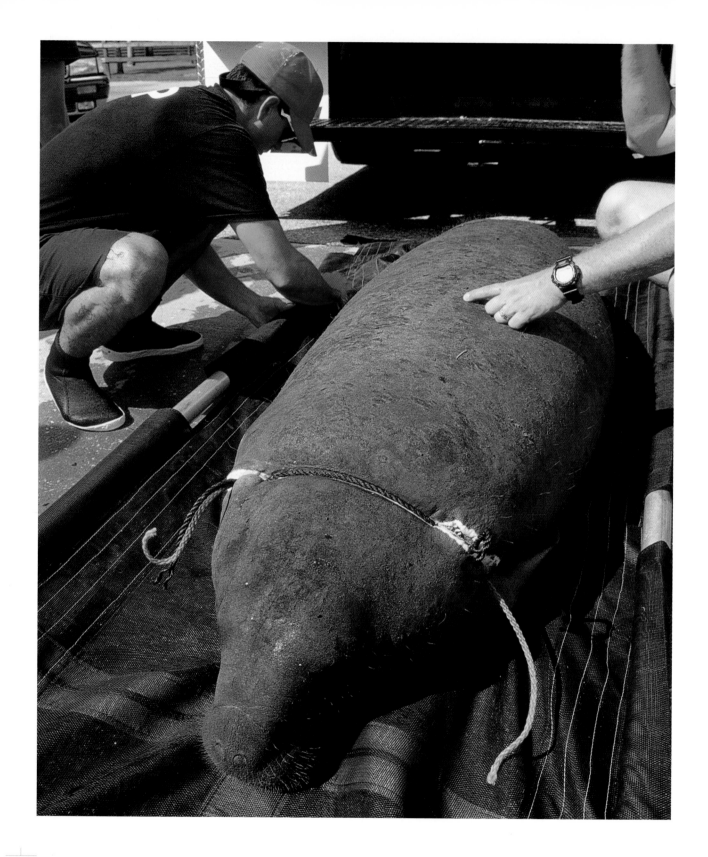

In the Company of Manatees

manatees but schools of warmth-loving fish. During the winter, the survival of many manatees depends on their access to the effluvial waters. Yet in Brevard County, boat-loads of fishermen motor among the animals, casting their lines right over the animals' backs to get at the fish.

"Of course boaters don't like to be banned from anywhere, and fishermen don't like it a lot because good manatee habitat is also excellent for fishing," says the Sirenia Project's Thomas O'Shea. "But if you want to save manatees, we have to make the choices."

"Paradoxically," wrote a columnist from Bogotá's *El Tiempo* newspaper (February 9, 1997), "the manatee is the fishermen's best friend, since it helps preserve the fauna of the places where it lives, including the fish. Its ecological and economic importance is directly proportional to its gluttony. . . . If the manatees are exterminated, [floating plants] grow to excess, impede the passage of light, and kill off microscopic algae that produce oxygen. This . . . reduces fishery production, which harms the very fishermen who contribute to the manatee's demise."

Litter

Debris tossed into Florida's waterways is more than unsightly. Discarded fishing line, hooks, plastic six-pack holders, plastic bags, abandoned crab-trap lines, and commercial hoop nets routinely cause injury and death to manatees. The curious, roving animals get entangled in coils of monofilament, accidentally ingest fishing hooks, and swallow litter left floating among the aquatic plants on which they feed. Manatee flippers have become so badly crippled from the binding effects of rope and monofilament that the deformities show up in their misshapened bones. Other animals have lost flippers, bones and all.

Sirenia Project biologists found plastic bags, string, rope, wire, rubber bands, and fishing line in the stomachs of 14.4 percent of 439 manatees recovered between 1978 and 1986. Monofilament fishing line was the most common item ingested, and in some cases it killed the animals when it blocked their digestive system. A few animals died when wire perforated their stomach lining.

"Other kinds of marks on carcasses include those caused by the manatee being scraped or rolled along the bottom while trapped under a hull or squeezed between a hull and the wall of a canal lock chamber."

—SCOTT WRIGHT, *pathologist, Florida Department of Environmental Protection*

Floodgates

South Florida is loaded with water-control structures. While they improve the quality of life for humans by controlling water levels throughout the state, the structures have been tough on native wildlife and wetland ecosystems. Manatees occasionally get crushed when floodgates and canal locks are closed, and mothers and calves have been separated by the man-made structures. In turn, when the gates are opened, the rush of outpouring water creates such tremendous suction that manatees often drown when they get pinned underwater.

To address these problems, the South Florida Water Management District and the U.S. Army Corps of Engineers are working together to improve the technology

ABOVE: *Power plants in Florida and Georgia attract manatees in search of warm water. Many of the plants offer staffed manatee viewing areas and public education centers to help promote wildlife conservation. (Photo courtesy the Florida Power & Light Company)*

used to open and close the floodgates. Options being considered include automatic reversal mechanisms and sonar devices to detect the presence of manatees near structure doors.

Power Plants

Long before Europeans arrived, manatees wintered in the warmer coastal waters of southern Florida and in several natural springs found on both sides of the peninsula. However, with the construction of hydroelectric power plants in Florida and southern Georgia as early as the 1940s, manatees began using the warm artificial habitats created by power-plant outfalls to extend their winter range farther north.

Every winter, this puts the effluent-dependent manatees at risk during power failures and severe temperature drops when even the power plants can't keep the manatees warm enough. At several of these man-made locations, where manatee forage areas have been lost to development and overgrazing, the animals readily trade access to food for warmth. But during severe cold spells, when manatees need food to help maintain their metabolism, they either must go without or must travel great distances to obtain it. Both situations can expose the animals to fatal cold stress.

Pollution and Water-Management Problems

Most of the environmental problems in southern Florida relate to water. One of the biggest concerns is the quality of water entering the Everglades' environment. Without enough clean water, in the right place at the right time, the Everglades and the rest of South Florida are threatened. Not only do all plants and animals in the area rely on water from the Everglades to survive, but so do people.

The Everglades are nothing more than a wide, slow-moving, shallow river. Like the manatees, they are believed to be millions of years old. Historically, the river once flowed undisturbed over a 100-mile expanse of subtropical wilderness at the meandering rate of ¼ to ½ mile a day from Lake Okeechobee south to the waters of Florida Bay and the Gulf of Mexico. The 40-mile-wide River of Grass extended from the highlands of the Atlantic Coastal Ridge westward into what is now Big Cypress National Preserve.

Each year there was a natural ebb and flow of water between the winter dry season and the rainy season, which begins in May. Left undisturbed, the wetlands of the Everglades supported a variety of plants and animals uniquely adapted to low nutrient levels and the naturally occurring fluctuations in water levels. This remarkable ecosystem remained intact until the late 1800s.

Since then the Everglades have been drained, diked, dissected by canals, converted into agricultural lands, and polluted with nitrates, phosphates, highway runoff, improperly treated sewage, and mercury. Floodgates were opened and closed with no regard for the natural water cycles of the native plants and animals.

An estimated 261 billion gallons of water once drained through the Everglades to South Florida's Atlantic coast each year. By 1992, more than 1,400 miles of canals were draining an additional 717 billion gallons of water from this precious ecosystem. Such severe habitat alterations have had a frightening impact on the Everglades, particularly on the wildlife of Everglades National Park. In less than 50 years, 90 percent of the park's magnificent wading bird populations have disappeared. Most noticeable are the wood storks, which numbered 150,000 in Florida in the early 1900s. By 1986 only 11,600 "flint heads" remained—in the Everglades and Cape Sable area.

Even more disturbing, in 1989 an autopsy performed on an endangered Florida panther found dead in the Shark River Slough area revealed that the cat's liver contained an elevated mercury level of 110 parts per million (ppm). According to the U.S. Food and Drug Administration, mercury levels above 1 ppm are considered unsafe. Peat or muck soils, such as those found in the Everglades, accumulate mercury. When the soils are mixed or disturbed—as during dredging and canal construction—they release the metallic toxin.

Phosphorus is the issue in the 500,000-acre Everglades Agricultural Area south of Lake Okeechobee. The Everglades' rich muck soil is naturally high in phosphorus. When the marsh is drained to grow vegetables and sugarcane, the soil oxidizes, adding phosphorus to runoff that enters the surrounding marshland. This nutrient infusion makes it possible for invading columns of cattails and other plants to eliminate the native saw grass.

The reduced flow of freshwater from Lake Okeechobee through the Everglades, diced with pollutants, has also had a dramatic effect on the plant and animal life of Florida Bay. In the area called the Dead Zone, dead and dying seagrass has covered acres of once lucrative shrimp and lobster breeding grounds with rotting muck, sponge beds have died, and once green mangroves have turned gray and lifeless. During summer, plumes of algae often spread for miles across waters that were once clear.

"The magnitude of the problem is immense," says marine biologist John E. Reynolds, chairman of the Marine Mammal Commission. "Almost any human activity in any inshore body of water or wetland in Florida can and does harm manatees or their habitat."

A Floating Food Source

For centuries, indigenous people throughout the historic range of the Sirenia have killed these benign animals for their meat, oil, and skin. Today, despite national and international laws that make this illegal, native communities outside the United States continue to hunt the endangered mammals throughout most of their remaining range. For example, "in Belize," says environmental writer Chris Wille, "sea cows are often seen as a bonanza of slow-moving steaks."

"The prescription for Florida Bay is clear but costly. Proposals to restore a significant flow of fresh water through the Everglades start at around $1 billion. But the cost of doing nothing could be even higher."

༺ཊ༻

—SPENCER REESE, *in* Newsweek, *November 2, 1992*

According to Wille, conservationists understand that endangered animals cannot be protected by laws when people are hungry and far from law enforcement. Under these conditions, financial incentives work better than punishment to encourage conservation. Hunters and poachers typically make the best nature guides—as soon as their illegal prey generates more income as a tourist attraction than as a main dish. As demonstrated in the Caribbean, the best way to reduce manatee poaching is to develop successful tourist programs that take people to see them in the wild. With visitors willing to pay $70 per person to catch a glimpse of a manatee in nature, no poacher wants to be socially ostracized as the "jerk" who lost his village's lucky lottery ticket.

"Docility, delicious flesh, and a low reproductive capacity are not beneficial characteristics for an animal," says World Wildlife Fund, Canada. "While hunting is now banned and all three species of manatees are protected under the Convention on International Trade in Endangered Species of Flora and Fauna [CITES], the threat from illegal hunting continues."

For example, in February 1997, 16 fishermen took half a day to corral, net, and club to death four of six remaining manatees in the El Llanito marsh in Santander, Colombia. Two of the animals were a cow and a calf. Those responsible for the slaughter then held a big manatee roast during which the two tons of poached meat fed more than 100 villagers, including the town police inspector.

Other Threats

Since Hurricane Andrew played havoc with South Florida in 1992, a small Air Force base located just 15 miles from Everglades National Park and 2 miles from Biscayne Bay National Park has remained closed. Now the shuttered facility is about to come to life. The Defense Department plans to lease the old base to Dade County for the next 20 to 30 years so that it can be converted into a regional airport. An environmental impact statement (EIS) was prepared for the proposed project in 1994. But since then, the project has been expanded into a huge international airport, with an estimated 230,000 flights per year anticipated by 2015. Instead of it being used as a backup to Miami International Airport, located 29 miles to the north, the new airport could very well turn into direct competition.

Environmentalists are concerned that the resulting noise and pollution generated by this venture will have devastating effects on the Everglades and surrounding wildlife habitats. The federal government is now conducting a supplemental EIS on the expanded facility.

Red Tide

During the first five months of 1996, an estimated 279 manatees died in Florida. It was a devastating number—more than 10 percent of the state's 2,639 manatees counted in a survey at the beginning of the year. One hundred and fifty of the deaths occurred

"Whether hurricanes have killed manatees is not known. Hurricane Elena forced saltwater into the Crystal River system in September 1985 and caused a reduction of freshwater aquatic plants (especially *Hydrilla),* which is the [manatee's] primary food in winter. Hurricane Andrew stranded at least one live Florida manatee in August 1992."

—BRUCE ACKERMAN,
biologist,
Florida Department of
Environmental Protection

IN THE COMPANY OF MANATEES

during a three-month period along the Gulf Coast of Florida. To determine what had caused the sudden manatee die-off, more than 200 of the world's best-known experts teamed up to try to unravel the mysterious event.

Red tides (natural algal blooms) sporadically occur along Florida's Gulf Coast. In 1982 an outbreak of red tide in southwest Florida closed shellfishing waters in Lee, Charlotte, and Collier Counties. When 37 manatees died, scientists suspected that red tide was the cause, but they had not yet developed the laboratory techniques now used to prove it.

During the 1996 manatee die-off, Lemon Bay became known as the Hot Zone. It was here, in the waterways around Fort Myers, that most of the deaths occurred. Stricken animals could be seen thrashing about in the bay, some sideways, others upside down. The body count quickly climbed as bloated manatee bodies began to wash up on shore.

This was a big manatee crisis. It was the biggest, in fact, since annual mortality numbers for Florida's manatees were first tallied in 1974. Not only was the mysterious plague quickly killing the endangered animals, but it more than doubled the total number of dead manatees (203) recorded from the previous year.

Many of the animals that died were individually known to scientists through the statewide photo-identification catalog maintained by the Sirenia Project in Gainesville. The situation was particularly heartbreaking because manatees are such slow breeders: even under the best of circumstances, Florida's manatee population increases by only 5 to 8 percent each year—barely enough to break even with the manatee deaths that occur during a "good" year. The manatee die-off of 1996 showed how quickly a natural disaster can push an endangered species even further into the red.

LEFT: *The water turned "red" with the bloom of a single-celled dynoflagellate whose toxin kills fish and manatees.*

During the 1996 crisis, attempts were made to rescue the stricken animals. Many were so ill that they could barely breathe. Using backhoes, trucks, and help from the local fire department, four sick manatees were hauled out of Lemon Bay and taken to Tampa's Lowry Park Zoo, where they were placed in holding tanks. At risk of drowning because they were too weak to lift their nostrils to the surface, the manatees were fitted with life preservers to help keep their heads and bodies afloat.

During the die-off, manatee carcasses piled up at such an unprecedented rate that outdoor sheds were converted into makeshift manatee morgues where the carcasses were kept on ice until emergency necropsies could be performed. According to Dr. Scott Wright of the Department of Environmental Protection's Marine Mammal Pathobiology Laboratory in St. Petersburg, Florida, initial autopsies revealed long red and purple stripes in the lung tissue of many of the stricken animals, an indication of severe shock to the lungs.

The outbreak began to subside in May, but it was not until July, after extensive lab tests and tissue cultures were completed, that scientists could finally prove that red tide poisoning had, in fact, killed the manatees. Borrowing technology from human medicine, Dr. Gregory Bossart at the University of Miami Medical School conducted a series of double-blind lab tests that revealed the presence of potent brevetoxins (the toxins produced by the algae) in the phagocytic cells of the livers, kidneys, lungs, stomachs, and brains of the dead manatees. Even the manatees' stomach contents were loaded with the toxins.

"Red tide rarely moves so far and so intensely into inshore waters where manatees congregate," says University of Miami toxicologist Daniel Baden. "This particular epizootic was spurred by an unseasonably cold weather pattern, which brought a large number of manatees to Florida's warm Gulf Coast, while a strong northwest wind blew a potent strain of red tide deep into the manatees' feeding and refuge areas. These two unusual events, which occurred between March 3 and late April of 1996, were a deadly combination for the manatees."

Outbreaks of harmful algal blooms (HABs) in Florida are killing fish, alligators, coral, birds, and manatees, and threatening the health of people who come in contact with them. Although there is evidence of naturally occurring HABs in the fossil record, scientists are now concerned with their increased frequency, and the emergence of deadlier species.

According to cynobacteria expert Wayne Carmichael of Wright State University, "Water sources throughout the world are increasingly polluted with fertilizer runoff [and human sewage], which provides the nutrients for luxuriant blooms of algae. Potentially deadly algae and nontoxic algae are virtually indistinguishable, except through sophisticated biochemical testing."

The 1996 Florida manatee crisis called international attention to the risks associated with toxic algal blooms, but for centuries people have known that eating shellfish saturated with red algae can lead to an agonizing death. According to *Seattle Times* reporter Diedtra Henderson (September 30, 1997), "The neurotoxins act like stalled cars in the body's expressway, blocking the movement of sodium through the nerve-cell membranes. Impulses no longer travel between nerves and the brain. Humans don't know what hit them until a strange tingling numbs their lips and faces. A rapid-fire set of ailments—nausea, dizziness, listlessness—follow, sometimes leading to death."

Until recently, little was known about similar neurotoxins released by blue-green algae, the greenish scum that, in a nontoxic form, clogs freshwater lakes and reservoirs from Illinois to Antarctica. When 69 patients at a dialysis clinic in Brazil suddenly dropped dead of seizures and liver hemorrhage, Sandra Azevedo, a biologist and algae neurotoxins expert at Federal University of Rio de Janeiro, recognized the outbreak for what it was—the first conclusive evidence of human deaths from pond scum, or more scientifically, blue-green algae, the tiny cousins of the better-known saltwater "red tide." Blue-green algae neurotoxins have no antidote.

Underscoring the voracity of algae neurotoxins, a red tide hit Hong Kong in 1998, killing more than 1,500 tons of fish in just a few days—about half of all the fish bred in Hong Kong's coastal waters that year. The toxic algae cost Hong Kong's beleaguered fishing industry an estimated $31 million.

While scientists now have a test to diagnose red-tide poisoning in manatees and other animals, and much more experience treating it due to Florida's 1996 manatee die-off, what they don't have is a solution for one of the ever increasing causes of toxic algal blooms—human-caused pollution. More than 400 million gallons of nitrate- and phosphate-rich sewage are injected into Florida's deep Class 1 wells each day. Sewage from the wells is now beginning to seep into the Florida aquifer and discharge into coastal waters.

"I don't know if anyone is looking into the association between Class 1 well waste and harmful algal blooms, but for any source, including Class 1 wells, if it involves nutrient loading, you can get a HAB."

⁓

—JOHN BURNS,
biologist,
St. Johns Water
Management District

The federal government now takes algae seriously. In 1994 a multi-agency task force was established called the Ecology and Oceanography of Harmful Algal Blooms—to coordinate funding and research to fight the toxic algal outbreaks nationwide.

In May 1998, Susanne Schwartz, acting director of the EPA's Oceans and Coastal Protection Divisions, testified to Congress on the threat of toxic algae, and asked that a National Harmful Algal Bloom Research and Monitoring Strategy be developed. On November 13, 1998, President Clinton signed into law the Coast Guard Authorization Act of 1998, which includes multimillion-dollar funding for the Harmful Algal Bloom and Hypoxia Research and Control Act of 1998.

Manatee Viruses

As if 1996 hadn't been hard enough on Florida's manatee population, the following year researchers discovered the first cases of viral infections ever reported in manatees. Skin lesions appeared on two captive manatees along Florida's Gulf Coast. According to Dr. Gregory Bossart, a University of Miami pathologist and veterinarian at the Miami Seaquarium, the lesions were caused by the papillomavirus, a virus found in humans, cows, and other mammals but never before seen in manatees.

BELOW: *A manatee stricken with red tide poisoning in 1996 stayed afloat in a manatee-sized life preserver at the Lowry Park Zoo. (Photo courtesy the Lowry Park Zoo)*

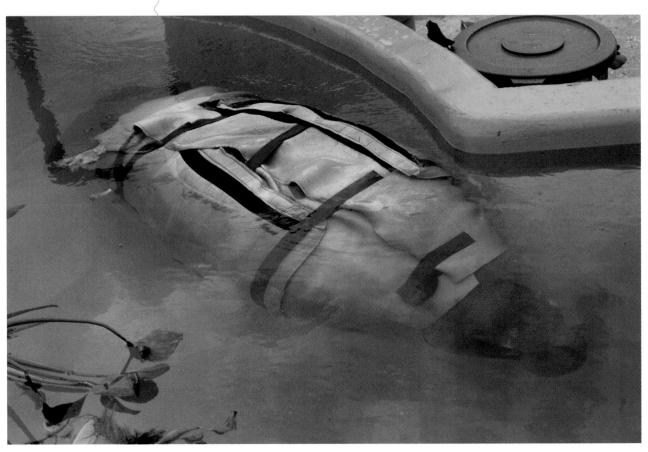

"I've always wondered how manatees can live in the Miami River, one of the most polluted rivers in America," said Dr. Bossart. "Manatees are superbly evolved to fight disease. So this raises a red flag."

Mark Lowe, a veterinarian at Homosassa Springs State Wildlife Park, first noticed the suspicious lesions under the eye of a resident eight-year-old female manatee. About the same time, a male manatee at the Lowry Park Zoo in Tampa developed similar lesions, followed by two other manatees at Homosassa Park.

Researchers don't know what caused the virus to show up in manatees, or how widespread it is. The papillomavirus is usually benign in other animals, although it can be transmitted. Seventy different papillomaviruses are found in people. More serious health problems can result when the virus causes tumors to develop near the eyes, nose, or genitals, affecting body functions.

"We've begun to see viral infections in other marine mammals," said Dr. Bossart. "Unrelated cases of malignant tumors have shown up in six bottlenose dolphins, and a viral infection similar to the one now found in manatees caused skin lesions in Keiko, the killer whale featured in *Free Willie*. This is a very disturbing development. Some strange [environmental] things are going on."

According to researcher Jan Boon of the Netherlands Institute for Marine Research, traces of toxic chemicals found in whales indicate that human-caused pollution is spilling deep into the Atlantic Ocean. Polybrominated chemical compounds were detected in the bodies of 13 minke and sperm whales that washed up on the Dutch coast in recent years. Because sperm whales feed at depths of 3,000 feet or more, the findings show that toxic pollution has spread farther into the ocean's food chain than previously thought.

As free-swimming barometers measuring the health of our marine environments, skin-lesioned sea creatures send a chilling message.

Energy Deregulation

"As if cold weather, red tides, and increasing numbers of watercraft weren't enough to worry about," adds Lynn Lefebvre, leader of the U.S. Geological Survey Sirenia Project, "manatees may soon be facing another problem: the disappearance or sporadic availability of warm water at sites north of their natural winter range. The proposed deregulation of Florida's power-plant industry may have profound effects on manatee mortality, distribution, and habitat use."

In the past, power plants have made every effort possible to protect the temperature-sensitive manatees with consistent power generation during the winter months. However, this may no longer be possible with deregulation, when consumer choice will determine which plants generate power, how often, and in what quantities. Hundreds of wintering manatees could be adversely affected if their effluvial habitats are suddenly reduced or eliminated.

"Every part of the earth is sacred to my people. Every shining pine needle, every sandy shore, every mist in the dark woods, every clearing and humming insect is holy in the memory and experience of my people.... The white man is a stranger who comes in the night and takes from the land whatever he needs. The earth is not his brother but his enemy.... Continue to contaminate your bed, and you will one night suffocate in your own waste."

∽

—CHIEF SEATTLE,
from a letter written in 1855 to President Franklin Pierce

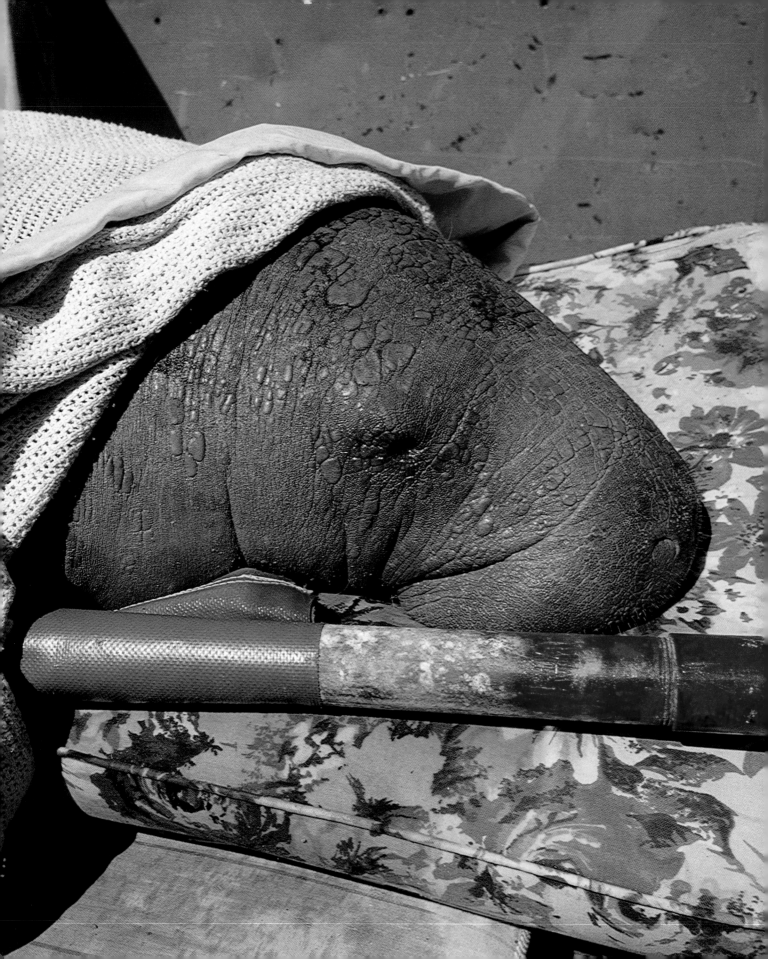

To Save an Endangered Species

According to manatee expert Thomas O'Shea, the Florida manatee has one of the longest records of protection for any species of wildlife in the New World. As early as the 1700s, England declared Florida a sanctuary for manatees in an attempt to control their slaughter. The decree was aimed at the Spanish smugglers and slave traders who were killing the animals by the boatload.

Commercial hunting of manatees in the 19th century depleted the Florida populations to such an extent that in 1893 the state passed the first laws to protect the animals. Fourteen years later, in 1907, fines were added—$500 and/or a six-month prison term for anyone caught molesting or killing a manatee. During the Depression and again during World War II, manatees were heavily poached for food. Many more subsequently died during the dynamiting of rock to deepen Florida's coastal water channels after the war.

Even so, it was not until the mid-1960s that the public finally began to show any remorse for a dead manatee. Until then, all that was known about these unobtrusive, mostly invisible marine mammals had been gleaned from lab dissection, the study of skeletal remains, and random observations in the wild. The animals had yet to take on a public persona that would endear them to the masses.

Then the situation began to change. In 1966 the Endangered Species Preservation Act passed. The following year, the West Indian manatee received official listing under the act, and Daniel Hartman began his pioneering study of manatee ecology and behavior in Crystal River.

In 1972, manatees received further protection under the Marine Mammal Protection Act. Under this federal law, not only is it illegal to capture a manatee without a valid permit, but if a manatee is harassed, injured, or killed, the offender may be fined. The more pervasive Endangered Species Act (ESA) of 1973 further increased the federal protection of manatees. Under the ESA it is illegal to "kill, hunt, collect, harass, harm, pursue, shoot, trap, wound, or capture an endangered species." Still in force, it authorizes agreements between states and the federal government and provides funding for management, research, and law enforcement. It also requires government agencies to review the potential impact to threatened habitats and species when planning construction projects.

Finally, in July 1978, the Florida Manatee Sanctuary Act was passed, designating the entire state of Florida a "refuge and sanctuary for manatees." Thirteen winter manatee protection zones were established and speed-zone signs posted. This act gives state officials the authority to enforce manatee protection, regulate boat traffic, designate speed zones, and confiscate the boats of convicted offenders. Boat speeds are now regulated in designated manatee areas from November 15 to March 31 each year. In the most critical areas, speed zones are effective year-round.

Anyone convicted of violating the Florida Manatee Sanctuary Act by intentionally or negligently annoying, molesting, harassing, or disturbing a manatee in any way, at any time, faces a possible maximum fine of $500 and/or imprisonment for up to 60 days. In circumstances of extreme harassment, such as severe injury or death to a manatee, the state of Florida has the right to pursue prosecution under federal law. Anyone convicted of violating the ESA or the Marine Mammal Protection Act faces stiffer penalties—fines up to $100,000 and/or one year in prison.

In fact, what began in the 1960s as a faint public curiosity about an oddball animal has now mushroomed into a major "manatee movement." Florida declared the West Indian manatee its official state marine mammal in 1975, and billboards depict the spoon-tailed animal as "the endangered Floridian." Visible throughout Florida on license plates, bumper stickers, T-shirts, postcards, real estate brochures, mugs, and posters, the sausage-shaped marine mammal now receives more press than a politician. From research, rehabilitation, and public education to lobbying and law enforcement, the manatee is a classic example of the tremendous mobilization of people and funds required to save an endangered species.

The Sirenia Project

For nearly a quarter of a century, the Sirenia Project, based in Gainesville, Florida, has planned and conducted research on the behavior, biology, population distribution, and conservation of the West Indian manatee. Initially established by the U.S. Fish and Wildlife Service and now managed by the U.S. Geological Survey, Biological Resources Division, the Sirenia Project encompasses a team of scientists dedicated to long-term research on the West Indian manatee in Florida. Staff biologists have carried out saltwater radio-tagging experiments and aerial population surveys and have scrutinized the manatee's diet, metabolism, migration routes, vocalizations, and social organization.

Photo Identification

Unfortunately, most of what is now known about manatee biology has resulted from the long-term recognition of individual animals made possible by their scars and deformities. "Most of the scars are from boats," says Cathy Beck, a Sirenia Project biologist who has worked with manatees since 1978, "prop scars, boat wounds, or tails partially chopped off."

Since the 1970s, researchers have used manatee scar patterns and mutilations like human fingerprints to identify individual animals. The Sirenia Project maintains the Manatee Individual Photo-identification System—an interactive photo-CD-based computer database developed with Ron Osborn of the U.S. Geological Survey. The

"Society should not stand for the extinction of a species any more than it should stand for the desecration of some great sculpture. The earth becomes a little less healthy, and we all become a little less human."

❧

—THOMAS O'SHEA,
*former project leader,
USGS Sirenia Project*

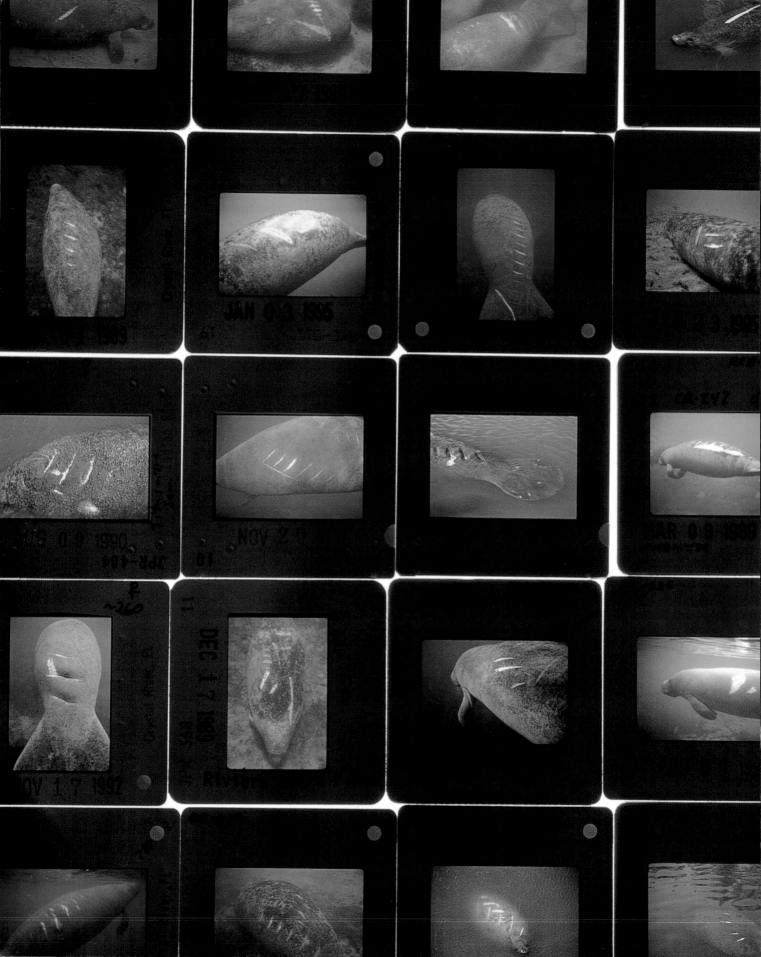

continually updated, computerized database has made it possible to document reproductive rates, adult survival rates, and the complex seasonal movement patterns of Florida manatees. Photographing and cataloging individual manatees over many years has contributed to the understanding of the species' behavior, movements, and life history. It has also developed into a macabre collection of gruesome photographs documenting the damage inflicted on manatees by powerboats and discarded monofilament. As of 1999, more than 1,400 individual manatees had been entered into the computer database, most of them wounded or scarred by human activity.

Based on data initially obtained from the catalog, it appeared to researchers that some manatees along the Atlantic Coast migrate seasonally between the St. Johns River and southern Florida. This raised the possibility that summer sightings of manatees as far north as Cape Hatteras, North Carolina, were of animals that winter as far south as Miami. In 1994, Chessie the roving manatee subsequently proved that manatees do indeed migrate 1,200 miles, and more, up and down the Atlantic Coast.

"In recent years," says Sirenia Project biologist Galen Rathbun, "it was thought that sufficient protection for manatees could be achieved by implementing local management plans, such as the plan prepared for the Crystal River area. But if manatees are regularly moving along the entire length of Florida's eastern coast, and perhaps farther north into Georgia and the Carolinas, then governmental agencies, private industry, and conservation organizations will have to reassess their strategies for protecting manatees and their habitat."

While the initial purpose of the manatee photo catalog was to learn about manatee reproduction rates and seasonal migration patterns, the computerized catalog now contains a database that documents manatee births and individual survival rates for almost a quarter century. These data, analyzed with recently developed statistical techniques, have made it possible for scientists at the U.S. Geological Survey in Gainesville and the National Center for Scientific Research in Montpellier, France, to calculate with greater accuracy the probability that an adult manatee will survive from one year to the next.

New estimates of long-term manatee survival suggest that some limited populations of the endangered animals may be growing, such as those found at Blue Spring and Crystal River. In contrast, the data also show that manatees inhabiting the state's more populated southeastern coast are not increasing and that their survival, in fact, appears precarious.

Aerial Surveys

Accurate manatee population counts are difficult to obtain. Florida and Georgia have more coastline (1,449 miles) than Washington, Oregon, and California combined (1,292 miles), and during summer, the manatees spread out over much of it. According to Florida Department of Environmental Protection biologist Bruce Ackerman, aerial surveys are a useful and cost-effective way to count manatees and for mapping mana-

"We all know that the time scale of evolution is in millions of years. Even changes in human demography are measured in decades and centuries, but wildlife management (really people management) is seldom planned more than a few years ahead."

〜

—CLAYTON RAY AND DARYL DOMNING, *in* Journal of Marine Mammal Science

tee distribution. They seem to be the only method by which large numbers of manatees in large areas can be counted. The surveys also provide detailed information on habitat use and have been used extensively to define areas that require legal protection.

"Most aerial surveys are conducted with a Cessna 172 or with a similar small, high-winged, four-seat airplane with good downward visibility," says Ackerman. "Flights are usually at an altitude of 150 m [490 feet] and at an airspeed of 130 km/h [80 mph]. When manatees are seen, the airplane slows and circles the area clockwise until the observer is reasonably sure that an accurate count was made."

According to Ackerman, high-resolution aerial video can be used to record sightings on long transects for later viewing and counting. Computer-image analysis can then be employed to detect and count manatees on videotapes and to measure body lengths. Finally, by using global positioning systems (GPS), researchers can improve the accuracy of sighting locations and accurately record the flight path to document the exact areas covered during flights.

Aerial surveys to count and map the distribution of Florida manatees have been used since 1967. At the beginning of 1996, statewide aerial surveys yielded population counts totaling 2,639 animals, the highest population count ever recorded for Florida manatees. In 1997 the aerial count dropped to 2,229: 416 manatees had died the previous year, almost half in the devastating red tide crisis.

There is nothing easy about coordinating a statewide aerial manatee survey. During two days in January 1998, observers from 13 agencies, universities, and research labs used 19 planes to make aerial surveys while 6 ground teams counted manatees that were not visible from the air in hidden waterways. They counted 2,022 manatees. The first of three statewide aerial surveys conducted in January 1999 counted 1,873 manatees. According to Bob Bonde, this low number reflects the fact that Florida had experienced a mild winter and the manatees were dispersed and more difficult to count.

Radio and Satellite Telemetry

With the arrival of warm spring weather, Florida manatees leave their winter refuges to disperse throughout the state and neighboring coastal waters, making observation and visual tracking difficult. In order to learn more about manatee behavior, the animals' seasonal migrations, and their use of critical habitat areas, scientists now use radio waves and satellite "eyes" to follow the manatees year-round in their fresh- and saltwater habitats.

Field scientists first began using radio waves to track manatees in the 1970s when they mounted a VHF (very high frequency) radio transmitter to a belt and then attached it to the base of a manatee's tail. However, the tracking device functioned well only in freshwater areas due to the corrosive nature of saltwater. And because the belt-mounted transmitter and antenna remained underwater with the manatee, scientists could detect the transmitter's radio signals only when the animal rose to the surface to breathe.

BELOW: *Sirenia Project biologist Galen Rathbun gently slips a tail collar around a Crystal River manatee.*

Biologists with the Sirenia Project helped solve a few of these problems in the early 1980s when they modified the radio-tag assembly and installed the VHF transmitter inside a watertight housing. Attached to the belt by a 6-foot-long flexible nylon tether, the housing was designed to float at the surface while the "subject" remained below. This enabled the radio transmitter to broadcast detectable VHF signals through the air—as long as the manatee remained submerged in shallow water. This technology is still used today.

"Trackers home in on the VHF signals using portable wildlife-tracking radio receivers, signal attenuators, and handheld directional 'H antennas,'" explains Charles ("Chip") Deutsch, a field biologist working with the Sirenia Project. "They also use Yagi antennas mounted on vehicles, boats, or aircraft. From light aircraft, scientists can locate VHF-tagged animals that are 20 to 30 miles away. However, most tracking is conducted from shore using handheld directional hydrophones and portable receivers that detect the signals at close range."

Radiotelemetry is a marked improvement over observing wildlife on a catch-as-catch-can basis. But because the technology offers a limited signal range, and requires biologists to physically chase the radio signals by foot and vehicle—the technology is time-consuming, costly, and often rife with logistical problems.

Then in 1985 manatee research went Space Age with the use of satellite telemetry when Bruce Mate assisted Sirenia Project biologists in designing a watertight, salt-water-resistant platform transmitter terminal (PTT) for manatees. The PTT was placed inside a larger cylindrical housing attached by tether to the tail belt with swivels to minimize drag. And should the tether snag, breakaway links were added to prevent the manatee from getting trapped. In 1987, VHF transmitters were incorporated in the PTT housings, and in 1988, an ultrasonic beacon was added to each housing to further help researchers locate manatees in the field.

Argos receivers onboard two polar-orbiting NOAA (National Oceanic and Atmospheric Administration) weather satellites receive the UHF (ultra-high-frequency) signals broadcast into space from the surface-floating PTT each time the satellites pass within "view" (within 2,500 km, or 1,550 miles) of a tagged manatee. During each 10-minute pass, PTT locations are calculated from the Doppler shift in the frequency of

the received signal as the satellite approaches and then moves away from the transmitter. The satellites pass over Florida an average of 9 times every 24 hours. Unbiased location data, received by satellite from the tagged animals, are then sent directly to Sirenia Project lab computers in Gainesville, Florida, via a global communications network. The process takes about twenty minutes from the moment the satellite picks up the transmitter message from the animal until it is downloaded to the biologist—who is often sitting hundreds, if not thousands of miles away from the tagged animal at his or her computer console.

The radio and the satellite tag assembly allows researchers to follow individual manatees for up to two years without causing harm or discomfort to the animal. Unique color band combinations at the top of each transmitter are used for visual identification of individual manatees.

"One of the major strengths of the Argos system," says Sirenia Project biologist Jim Reid, who helped track 83 tagged manatees along the Atlantic Coast from 1986 to 1996, "is that data collection is relatively systematic, continuing day and night regardless of inclement weather or an animal's location. Because manatees are slow moving and inhabit shallow waters, the tethered transmitter enables tracking in brackish and saltwater habitats. In addition, the tag is visible, allowing researchers to spot and observe study animals from a distance."

As a result of the tagging program, researchers have been able to record some interesting, if not surprising, manatee movements. One female manatee traveled between Fernandina Beach and Brevard Country seven times, making this 150-mile trip in less than four days on at least one occasion. The energetic female swam nearly 45 miles per day and traveled into the Atlantic Ocean and along the beach for several portions of her journey. Such rapid, long-distance movements had not previously been documented for individual manatees. Data obtained from the tagging program is now being used to help identify important manatee habitats along the Atlantic and Gulf coasts, and to establish additional manatee protection zones in Florida.

Captive Breeding

Unlike California condors and black-footed ferrets, whose ultimate survival has depended on successful captive-breeding programs, Florida's manatees are reproducing just fine on their own, albeit slowly. In fact, because the Florida manatee breeds so easily in captivity, in 1991 the U.S. Fish and Wildlife Service (USFWS) banned the mixing of sexes at captive facilities to prevent overcrowding.

While every effort is made to rehabilitate sick and injured manatees for release back into the wild, captive-bred and orphaned manatees raised in captivity have difficulty surviving in the wild. Unlike the condors and black-footed ferrets, manatees depend on a prolonged relationship with their mothers to learn the location of critical migration routes, feeding areas, and overwintering sites. Without this knowledge, a manatee doesn't have a fighting chance of surviving in the wild.

"Unlike manatees, dugongs have rarely been maintained in captivity and have never bred in captivity."

—HELENE MARSH,
biologist,
James Cook University

"The number of carcasses recovered each year continues to increase, and so does public concern for the future of the Florida manatee."

☙

—GALEN RATHBUN,
*former project leader,
USGS Sirenia Project*

In 1984, SeaWorld Orlando veterinarian Jesse White placed two captive-bred manatees in holding pens at Homosassa River; two years later he released them when they appeared capable of feeding themselves. Because there were never any confirmed follow-up sightings of the pair, the USFWS eventually pronounced them dead.

"It's like taking a pet and releasing it into the forest," USFWS manatee recovery coordinator Robert Turner told Craig Quintana of the *Orlando Sentinel*. "They have no experience at all on anything but romaine lettuce in a concrete tank. When [they run] out of lettuce, [they don't] eat. We just thought they'd start eating other vegetation."

In 1994, SeaWorld Orlando and the USFWS set up a $40,000 4.5-acre "halfway station" for manatees in the Banana River between Cape Canaveral and the Kennedy Space Center as a place where manatees could acclimatize to a natural diet of seagrass before being released. As part of this "soft release" program, manatees are weighed each month to monitor how well they are adjusting. As of 1998, nearly 50 manatees were in captivity at five captive maintenance facilities in Florida.

Manatee Salvage and Rescue Program

"Understanding the causes of manatee injury and death is critical to enable implementation of strategies to minimize these threats," says David Arnold, chief of the Bureau of Protected Species Management, Florida Department of Environmental Protection (FDEP).

To this end, the FDEP coordinates the Manatee Salvage and Rescue Program at the Florida Marine Mammal Pathobiology Laboratory (MMPL), located in St. Petersburg. The program is responsible for collecting and examining virtually all manatee carcasses reported in the southeastern United States. Necropsy results enable FDEP staff to determine the causes of death, monitor mortality trends, and disseminate mortality information needed to help protect the animals in the wild.

Biologist husband-and-wife team Bob Bonde and Cathy Beck of the Sirenia Project remember a particularly gruesome recovery they experienced—that of a carcass lodged in a discharge pipeline at a Jacksonville generating plant. Access to the decomposing carcass was through a 48-inch manhole. Bonde and fellow project biologist Galen Rathbun descended into the pipe to free the dead animal. Although plant workers complained of the stench, says Rathbun, it was the 10 gallons of Lysol they poured into the manhole that was far worse.

And some recoveries have been sad. In June 1996 an adult female manatee was found dead in a canal near Fort Lauderdale. Using descriptions of her scar patterns and the numbers on her radio-tracking belt, the scientists realized that this was TBC-09, an individual they had tracked since 1987 and affectionately called "C-cow."

"After having learned many of the intimate details of C-cow's life and interacting with her in the field over the past nine years," says Bonde, "we felt as if we had lost a close friend. We hope that the insights into manatee biology she provided will be used for appropriate and effective measures to protect manatees in Florida."

By doing necropsies on dead animals, FDEP scientists identify some of the causes of mortality, while gathering valuable natural-history information such as the animal's gender, weight, length, approximate age, stomach contents, and pathology. The cause of death is divided into categories and quantified so researchers can better understand the ongoing threats to manatee survival. The Manatee Salvage and Rescue Program has also helped identify high-use, high-risk areas in Florida that should be designated as manatee sanctuaries.

So what do you do with a half-ton dead manatee after it has been necropsied? "For the past five years we have incinerated carcasses at the Marine Mammal Pathobiology Lab," says DEP scientist Tom Pitchford. According to Pitchford, operational costs for the incinerator, including natural gas, maintenance, repair, and permits, are estimated at $15,000 a year. Recently, DEP has begun using the free services of a local rendering plant to collect and dispose of the carcasses and other animal by-products. "We like the idea of recycling the manatee carcasses into usable dry protein products and liquid tallow rather than seeing them go up in smoke," says Pitchford. "This way we are returning their energy to the environment instead of using natural gas."

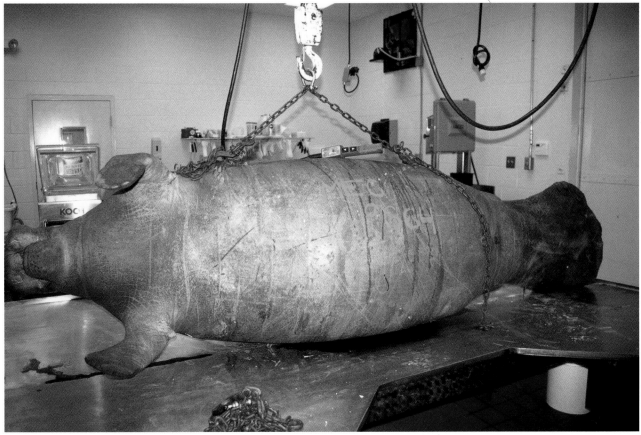

Florida Department of Environmental Protection

According to FDEP field biologist Tom Pitchford, the manatee protection program is a top priority at the department because the manatees face such a host of problems, most of them man-made. By far the most serious threat to their survival is the loss of habitat.

"Manatees graze on seagrass meadows," says Pitchford. "Pollution of coastal waters, rivers, and canals is partly the result of land development. With Florida's expected increase in population, the manatee's habitat will become even more degraded."

"The habitat issue promises to ultimately dwarf motorboat speed rules in complexity, controversy and duration," wrote William Sisson *(Soundings,* July 1994), "because it's linked to so many land-use and development questions."

In the meantime, one of the primary goals of the FDEP is to add to the manatee protection zones where speed limits and marine patrols help keep the animals safe from divers, boats, and barges. In 1989, as a result of the increasing number of manatee deaths due to boat collisions, Florida's governor, Bob Martinez, and his cabinet identified 13 "key" counties where more than 80 percent of all manatee deaths were occurring: Dade, Collier, Lee, Sarasota, Broward, Palm Beach, Martin, St. Lucie, Indian River, Brevard, Citrus, Volusia, and Duval. The FDEP was asked to work with each of the counties to help develop Manatee Protection Plans that would address the multitude of threats facing the animals. Each county government was also asked to develop site-specific boat speed zones.

RIGHT: *A crowd of people helps to rescue an orphaned baby manatee. (Photo courtesy the Florida Department of Environmental Protection/ Tom Pitchford)*

The Florida Marine Patrol

Florida has roughly 8,400 miles of tide-affected waters, 11,900 miles of inland rivers and streams, 10,000 miles of canals, and 3,000,000 acres of man-made and natural lakes. The vastness of this aquatic system makes it difficult for a few hundred officers of the Florida Marine Patrol (FMP) to enforce speed regulations on the state's waterways. Yet enforce the laws they do, particularly the state and federal laws affecting manatees.

The public can help by lending their eyes and ears to the FMP. A toll-free Manatee Hot Line (1-800-DIAL-FMP) makes it possible for anyone who observes a manatee in trouble to pick up the phone and call for help. The public is asked to phone in reports of sick, injured, orphaned, and dead manatees, as well as sightings of healthy animals fitted with radio tags used in satellite-telemetry research. Most important, if you witness a manatee being harassed or abused in any way, pick up the phone and call. Quick action may save the life of a manatee—and lead to the capture of the offender.

Wildlife officials coordinate the rescue of sick, injured, or orphaned manatees as needed. Three critical-care treatment facilities in Florida are authorized to capture, transport, and treat sick or injured manatees under the joint supervision of the U.S. Fish and Wildlife Service and the Florida Department of Environmental Protection: Lowry Park Zoo, Miami Seaquarium, and SeaWorld Orlando. The DEP's Florida Marine Research Institute (FMRI), located in St. Petersburg, also helps supervise the rescue and transportation of manatees around the state, both dead and alive.

Ironically, it is the owners of Florida's more than 800,000 registered boats who help pay for the state's much-needed manatee research and conservation efforts—through a percentage of their annual registration fees.

U.S. Fish and Wildlife Service

A species is endangered when it is considered in immediate danger of extinction. Since 1967, the West Indian manatee has been listed by the U.S. Fish and Wildlife Service (USFWS) as endangered throughout its range. In fact, it is one of the most endangered marine mammals in coastal waters of the United States. Florida manatees constitute the largest known group of West Indian manatees anywhere in the species' range.

Based on a thorough assessment of the situation, the USFWS published the revised Florida Manatee Recovery Plan in 1995 as a statewide guide for the protection and recovery of this endangered species. According to the document, "mortality data collected since 1974 indicate a clear increase in manatee deaths over the last 15 years. Increasing numbers of manatees killed by boats and tremendous increases in boat traffic are the most important problem presently faced by manatees in Florida. Intensive coastal development is perhaps the greatest long-term threat to the Florida manatee. Their survival will depend on maintaining the integrity of ecosystems and habitat sufficient to support a sustainable manatee population."

The Florida Manatee Recovery Plan outlines a list of actions needed to protect the

"In the pursuit of economic gain, most people do not want to be bothered by questions about biodiversity."

—JOHN B. COBB, JR.,
*Professor of Theology,
Claremont University*

endangered mammals. As part of a designated Manatee Recovery Team, Save the Manatee Club (SMC) carries out the tasks specified in the plan under the auspices of the USFWS and makes recommendations to the head of the Florida Department of Environmental Protection on manatee issues.

For example, for several years, the Marine Mammal Commission and SMC had asked for a manatee sanctuary at Three Sisters Spring in Crystal River, Florida. Described as a "petting zoo," the spring attracted not only manatees but thousands of divers who routinely harassed the resting manatees by surrounding them to pet, touch, sit on, and even stand on them.

Local Crystal River dive-shop owners, concerned for the welfare of the manatees, approached the Citrus County government in hopes of getting an ordinance passed to establish a new sanctuary at Three Sisters Spring, only to find that such a decision is under the jurisdiction of Crystal River. When the city failed to take timely action on the sanctuary request, the USFWS stepped in and implemented an emergency sanctuary at Three Sisters during the winter of 1998. The USFWS is now moving forward to obtain a permanent sanctuary ruling for Three Sisters Spring.

The USFWS also teamed up with SMC to develop a waterproof educational decal that can be affixed to boat consoles within eyesight of the driver. Printed with special ink to withstand the elements, the free two-color decal, called "Please Watch for Manatees—Operate with Care," gives tips to boaters on how to reduce manatee deaths and injury from watercraft collisions and other human activities.

"Even under the best of conditions, manatees can be hard to spot in Florida's waterways," says SMC's executive director, Judith Vallee. "This decal goes on the boat and out with the boater, so it is right there to remind boaters how to watch for manatees and what to do if they spot an injured manatee. It's our hope the decal will help to get Florida's boating public more involved in helping to protect these unique animals."

The National Wildlife Refuge System

At the beginning of the twentieth century, President Theodore Roosevelt was deeply troubled that America's wildlife was disappearing at an alarming rate. "Wild beasts and birds are by right not the property merely of the people who are alive today," said our 26th president, "but the property of unborn generations, whose belongings we have no right to squander."

So moved, Roosevelt took action to protect our native wildlife. In 1903, Florida's Pelican Island became our nation's first wildlife refuge. Others followed. Thanks to Roosevelt's pioneering conservation efforts at the turn of the century, his vision subsequently evolved into today's National Wildlife Refuge System. Administered by the U.S. Fish and Wildlife Service, the system now comprises over 500 refuges and more than 92 million acres of protected lands and waterways across all 50 states and many U.S. terri-

"There is a movement afoot in the United States that environmentalists call deep ecology. In a nutshell, its basic tenet is that all living things have a right to exist— that human beings have no right to bring other creatures to extinction or to play God by deciding which species serve us and should there- fore be allowed to live. . . . Deep ecology is similar to many Eastern religions in holding that all living things are sacred."

—JAMES D. NATIONS, *Conservation International*

tories. Among these are several refuges that protect manatees in Florida: Merritt Island National Wildlife Refuge, Lower Suwannee National Wildlife Refuge, Cedar Keys National Wildlife Refuge, Crystal River National Wildlife Refuge, Hobe Sound National Wildlife Refuge, J. N. "Ding" Darling National Wildlife Refuge, Caloosahatchee National Wildlife Refuge, and Chassahowitzka National Wildlife Refuge.

The Army Corps of Engineers

The Department of the Army, Corps of Engineers (COE) is a federal agency that oversees water-resource development in the nation's rivers, lakes, harbors, and wetlands. The COE is responsible for maintenance of harbors and navigation channels, including the Intracoastal Waterway, a major migration corridor for manatees.

Because canal locks and flood-control structures are hazardous to manatees (they can get crushed, drowned, or penned), the COE has taken steps to try to eliminate the dangers to manatees in Florida's water-control system. Gate operation is controlled and timed, and special manatee barriers have been constructed to discourage manatees from entering the canal locks and floodgates.

Hydroelectric Power Plants

Florida Power and Light (FPL) has a challenging job—that of meeting the growing energy needs of customers in one of the most popular tourist and retirement states in the nation while minimizing environmental impacts on Florida's rich natural resources, wildlife, and scenic beauty. Over the years, FPL has done an excellent job demonstrating that utility plants can be built and operated compatibly with the environment—that industry and the environment can share resources in a manner that is beneficial to both. The best example of this is FPL's ongoing relationship with the state's endangered manatee population.

FPL operates 13 power plants across its service territory. Manatees congregate in the warm-water outflow at 5 of these plants during the winter months: Cape Canaveral, Fort Lauderdale, Port Everglades, Riviera Beach, and Fort Myers. As part of an ongoing public-awareness effort, FPL produces a series of educational brochures on different aspects of the environment affected by the company's operations, including a booklet specifically on the West Indian manatee.

"These artificially heated sources have conditioned manatees to expect warm water," says marine biologist John E. Reynolds, "so that many manatees now remain north of their historic wintering grounds. At each of four plants (Cape Canaveral, Riviera, Port Everglades, and Fort Myers), more than 200 manatees have been counted in single aerial surveys during very cold weather."

Scientists now realize that these artificial habitats can put the animals at risk for three main reasons: (1) Most power plants are located in heavily developed areas of the state where adequate manatee forage no longer exists; (2) the temporary shutdown of a power plant during cold weather can result in manatee mortalities; and (3) during extremely cold weather fronts, even operational power plants may not be able to provide the warm water needed by the animals to survive.

As a result, FPL makes every effort possible to keep its plants running smoothly—for the sake of the manatees. "We have the obligation to help protect these manatees for at least two reasons," an FPL official says. "One, they are a precious and increasingly rare resource. And two, we need to prove we can build and operate the facilities necessary to bring you the power you demand, and protect the animals with which we coexist."

According to Save the Manatee Club, many of these discharge areas have still not been designated manatee sanctuaries. As a result, commercial fishing guides often disregard the posted idle speed limit to bring boatloads of paying customers into the discharge areas. The sheer number of boats and anglers casting onto the manatees (which huddle there for their survival) is harassment of the worst kind, according to Save the Manatee Club. A campaign is now under way to create "no entry" manatee sanctuaries at the power plants in Brevard County.

World Wildlife Fund

Scientists of the World Wildlife Fund (WWF) have identified 200 key "ecoregions," called the "Global 200," that are critically important for their rich diversity of species and other unique biological features. Among the 200 ecoregions identified around the planet is one that directly affects the well-being of Florida's manatee populations—Everglades Flooded Grasslands and Savannas.

According to WWF, lying between temperate and subtropical America, between freshwater and brackish water, between shallow bays and deeper coastal waters, the Florida Everglades have a diverse range of habitats. This is one of the world's only rain-fed flooded grasslands on limestone. The region contains some 11,000 species of seed-bearing plants, 25 varieties of orchids, both tropical (palms) and temperate (oak) tree species, and even desert plants such as cactus and yucca. The Everglades are home to more than 323 bird species, 150 fish species, and 400 species of land and water vertebrates, 36 of which are endangered. Species include Schaus' swallowtail, the Florida tree snail, the Roseate spoonbill, the Florida panther, the American crocodile, and the West Indian manatee. WWF is working with numerous other conservation groups to help the U.S. Army Corps of Engineers, the National Park Service, and other federal and state governmental partners to restore the natural water flows that are essential to this unique ecosystem.

The Nature Conservancy

"Our goal is to identify the remnant habitat of the most endangered species and ecosystem types," says Alexander Watson, vice president of The Nature Conservancy. "These are the last strongholds of species that are running out of time. The fact is, if you don't save these habitats, the endangered plant and animal species they harbor will simply be gone."

"We use manatees to help design marine reserves," explains Nature Conservancy

ABOVE: *Clustered tightly together in the warmth of a power plant's discharge, a group of manatees hugs the shore like tadpoles blackening the edge of a shallow spring pond. (Photo courtesy the USGS Sirenia Project)*

representative Will Heyman. "One of the many reasons to establish a reserve is to protect habitat for endangered species. Charismatic species such as manatees are good indicators of critical habitats, and they attract positive attention."

Working with the Toledo Institute for Development and the Environment (TIDE) and other conservation groups, The Nature Conservancy is helping to develop management plans for a proposed reserve along the southern coast of Belize. Once established, the Port Honduras Marine Reserve would benefit the largest herd of West Indian manatees in the Caribbean. During aerial surveys in 1994, biologists spotted 256 manatees along the coasts of Mexico and Belize, by far the highest count outside of Florida.

According to Heyman, the multiuse reserve will give impetus and structure to manatee research, public education, and law enforcement needed to save the endangered mammals. In turn, it is hoped that the increasing economic value of manatees as tourist attractions will help win political support for the new sanctuary.

Miami Seaquarium®

The Miami Seaquarium is a critical-care facility involved with the rescue, rehabilitation, and release of injured, sick, and orphaned manatees. In 1968, a staff veterinarian, the late Jesse White, helped rescue a male manatee that got stuck in a Florida storm drain. A manatee rescue team, aided by the Florida Department of Transportation, was able to chop up the drain and save the emaciated animal. Dubbed Sewer Sam, the lucky manatee was nursed back to health at the aquarium and released to the wild in 1971 as the star of a Jacques Cousteau *Undersea World* television special.

The aquarium has had many successful manatee rescues and releases since then. In May 1998—with help from a semitruck, two cranes, two forklifts, two helicopters, several boats, about thirty personnel, several different agencies, and a small contingency from the media—the aquarium released two captive-born and one orphaned manatee into Coot Bay in Everglades National Park.

For more than forty years, the Miami Seaquarium has promoted manatee research and public education programs. In 1998, more than 750,000 guests and schoolchildren passed through the aquarium's Endangered Manatee Exhibit, where staff gave more than 1,000 question-and-answer presentations, including the fact that manatees are lactose intolerant. As a result, the Miami Seaquarium has developed a special formula to feed their orphaned charges that consists of Isomil, goat's milk, multimilk, lactinex, and children's chewable vitamins. When asked to teach others how to bottle-feed and care for orphaned manatees, the veterinary staff, headed by Gregory Bossart, hand-carries this life-saving formula to aquariums located as far away as Mexico and Colombia.

SeaWorld Orlando

Every year, SeaWorld helps rescue hundreds of injured, beached, and stranded animals along the U.S. coasts. In fact, over the last *five* years, SeaWorld has rescued more than 3,000

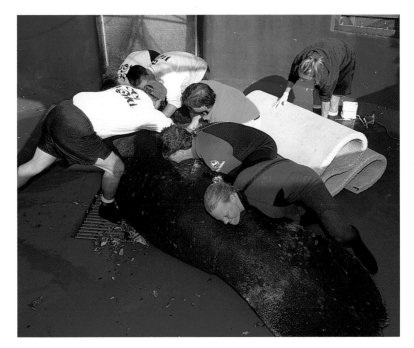

animals. The goal in these rescue efforts is to rehabilitate the animals, return them to the wild, and learn as much as possible to help in caring for future animals. As a result, researchers at the marine park have added to the body of scientific knowledge about a variety of animals, knowledge that could not have been obtained through studies in the wild.

As one of three critical-care treatment facilities involved with manatee rescue and rehabilitation in the state of Florida, SeaWorld Orlando undertakes rehabilitation on sick and injured manatees, conducts necropsies on carcasses taken through the manatee salvage program, and provides public education about the plight of the manatee through its award-winning exhibit "Manatees: The Last Generation?" Since it launched its Manatee Rescue and Rehabilitation program in 1976, the park's marine mammal rescue team has recovered more than 230 manatees from Florida waters and released 87 back into the wild after rehabilitation.

When an injured, 1,300-pound female manatee named Fathom was brought to SeaWorld's rehabilitation facility in 1991, she was fitted with a specially designed wet suit to help her survive a collapsed lung and broken ribs suffered in a boat collision. The neoprene wet suit, possibly the largest ever made, was designed by SeaWorld animal-care staff and handmade by Fathom Dive Suits of Orlando—hence the manatee's name. A special pocket on the outside of the wet suit could be filled with varying amounts of high-density foam to adjust Fathom's buoyancy so she could breathe and eat.

SeaWorld's commitment to conservation is evident in their ongoing work in animal rescue and rehabilitation, captive breeding, medical care, scientific studies, and innovative public education. "The importance of these programs becomes even greater as the activities and by-products of modern society increasingly threaten the natural habitats of thousands of species," says a SeaWorld spokesperson.

ABOVE LEFT: *Seven people, attempting to roll an injured manatee on its side at SeaWorld, clearly show the effort involved in moving such a hefty animal. (Photo © 1999 SeaWorld Orlando)*

ABOVE: *Two SeaWorld manatees haul themselves over the edge of their tank to meet a group of schoolchildren—and eat a bit of lettuce. (Photo © 1999 SeaWorld Orlando)*

Tampa's Lowry Park Zoo

Lowry Park's Florida Manatee Hospital and Aquatic Center is one of three critical-care facilities for the Florida manatee. Funded by Pepsi Cola and the city of Tampa, the $3.3 million hospital and aquatic center has rehabilitated and released nine manatees since it opened in 1991. Here, ill and injured manatees can be X-rayed and can undergo surgery with anesthesia in an operating room equipped just like in a hospital for humans.

The rehabilitation area consists of three 16,500-gallon concrete tanks, which can hold up to 16 manatees. Heater and chiller units allow for treatment of, respectively, hypothermic or hyperthermic rehabilitation cases, and the facility also conducts studies of manatee metabolism and bioenergetics. As at the Miami Seaquarium and SeaWorld Orlando, the goal at Lowry is to treat a sick or injured manatee's medical problem, allow it time to recover, and then, if possible, return it to the wild.

Homosassa Springs State Wildlife Park

Managed by the Florida Department of Environmental Protection, Division of Recreation and Parks, Homosassa Park serves as a rehabilitation center and refuge for manatees that have been orphaned or injured in the wild or have been born in captivity. The natural-spring environment allows them to acclimatize to a more natural environment before they are returned to the wild. In the process, they are delightful participants in the park's public education programs on Florida's endangered wildlife.

RIGHT: *Edmund and Laura Gerstein studied manatee hearing abilities for many years at the Lowry Park Zoo. (Photo courtesy the Lowry Park Zoo)*

Florida Audubon Society

With more than 30,000 members, the Florida Audubon Society is the oldest conservation organization in Florida. They held their first meeting in 1900 and were incorporated in 1902. An established leader in natural-resource protection, conservation issues, and environmental education, the society works closely with other groups involved in manatee protection. In fact, Save the Manatee Club began as a nonprofit affiliate of the Florida Audubon Society in 1981.

Corporate Help

In addition to the more than 8,000 acres of the Walt Disney World Resort's 30,500-acre property which have been designated as conservation lands, Disney has preserved another parcel of critical Florida habitat. Just 15 miles south of the Magic Kingdom, 8,000 acres of woods and wetlands at the headwaters of the Everglades were purchased by Disney and donated to The Nature Conservancy, along with funds for property management and an on-site education/administration center. Preserving a big chunk of Florida's natural history, this wilderness oasis is home to bald eagles, sandhill cranes, gopher tortoises, wood storks, and bobcats. Indigo snakes sunbathe on knobby cypress knees (roots) as nearby alligators digest their turtle and speckled perch meals. The Disney Wilderness Preserve also serves as a living laboratory for research scientists and students as they restore parts of the land once used for turpentining and cattle ranching.

Meanwhile, over in Fort Myers, Radisson Inn Sanibel Gateway is making "Manatee Magic" in partnership with Save the Manatee Club (SMC) in an effort to raise public awareness about the endangered animals. Radisson guests are greeted by a letter from the manager that outlines the "Manatee Magic" public education campaign and explains how hotel guests can help. The hotel set up an SMC traveling manatee display in the reception area and converted the lobby fountain into a "Make a Manatee Wish" wishing well, with all coins donated to SMC. "Make a Manatee Difference" paper-money receptacles placed at the hotel's front desk and restaurant make it easy for guests and patrons to donate funds to manatee conservation. The enthusiastic Radisson staff even adopted several of the manatees in SMC's Adopt-A-Manatee program (see page 157) and encouraged hotel guests to do the same.

Florida's Effort to Save the Manatee

Not only is the West Indian manatee Florida's official marine mammal, but November has been designated as the state's Manatee Awareness Month. Continuing conservation efforts include public acquisition and creation of manatee sanctuaries, ongoing field research, the establishment of additional regulatory speed zones,

"Whatever natural extinctions took place before the presence of humans is irrelevant, because today we are such a dominant species that theoretically we have the understanding and the power to stop or at least to mitigate our destruction of the natural world."

∽

—DAVID CHALLINOR,
Senior Scientist Emeritus,
Smithsonian Institution

increased public education programs, and expanded conservation management.

Under the Conservation and Recreational Lands (CARL) program, new areas containing important manatee habitat are being added to federally and state-protected areas. So far, more than $500 million has been spent to acquire 250,000 acres of land. Five percent of the CARL program budget is currently devoted to manatee-related purchases, including recent land acquisitions near Crystal River, Blue Spring, Rookery Bay, and the Sebastian River.

In addition, a state rule passed by the Marine Fisheries Commission in 1992 now makes it a second-degree misdemeanor to intentionally discard any monofilament fishing line or monofilament netting into or onto the waters of the state of Florida.

"The West Indian manatee in Florida waters is the perfect challenge for U.S. marine mammal conservation," wrote Clayton Ray and Daryl Domning. "Here is a population free of the hassles of international conflicts (such as whaling), subsistence pressures (as are the bowhead and dugong) and competition from commercial and recreational fisheries (such as tuna, salmon, abalone). They aren't dangerous (as are polar bears and mainland elephant seals). They are accessible, countable and well-known scientifically in comparison to most pinnipeds and cetaceans. Under proper conditions, they are tolerant of people at close range and are a proven tourist attraction; and they share their range with one of the most affluent, sophisticated and conservation-minded human populations in the world."

Save the Manatee Club

In 1981, responding to the need to help the endangered West Indian manatee, former Florida governor Bob Graham and singer-songwriter Jimmy Buffett joined forces to establish the nonprofit Save the Manatee Club (SMC). Based in Maitland, Florida, the club has as its primary purpose the promotion of public education, awareness, research, and grassroots lobbying efforts on behalf of the manatee. With more than 40,000 members from all over the world, the club makes use of an Adopt-A-Manatee program to raise funds to produce and distribute televised public-service announcements and manatee public-awareness waterway signs, to lobby legislators, to fund aerial manatee surveys, to purchase needed research equipment, and to conduct ongoing public-education programs. In 1994 the club even helped pay to fly Chessie the wayward male manatee (see page 89) home to Florida from Chesapeake Bay.

SMC has lobbied to add additional manatee sanctuaries, successfully restricted high-speed boat testing within manatee protection zones, and helped obtain boat speed limits in key manatee coastal counties. Club members such as model Cheryl Tiegs and television host Alex Trebek have helped to publicize the plight of the manatee. In 1997 another club member, payload commander Dr. Jan Davis, circled the earth aboard Space Shuttle Discovery on mission STS-85 with a Save the Manatee bumper sticker pasted visibly inside the cockpit.

The club also helped introduce and pass a bill authorizing the issue of manatee automobile license plates, which enables the public to make voluntary contributions

"There are many ways of seeing the biosphere. Our responses to nature—to the world—are as diverse as our personalities. Most experiences are quite ordinary, everyday encounters. But some experiences leave vivid memories and can change our behavior. These so-called peak experiences can fuse our separate selves to nature, establishing a lifetime bond."

∽

—MICHAEL E. SOULÉ,
Science Director,
The Wildlands Project

directly to the Florida Department of Environmental Protection (FDEP) through moneys collected in a Save the Manatee Fund. Donations generated from the manatee specialty plates not only help fund ongoing state conservation efforts, they also keep images of the endangered mammals highly visible on car bumpers. Since Florida started offering the special license plates at $15 each in 1990 (raised to $20 in 1999), the program has sold over 420,500 plates and generated more than $21.3 million for FDEP's manatee research program.

For many years SMC has also sponsored a manatee-sighting program to collect information on areas manatees use. Because research funds are limited, volunteer programs such as this are invaluable in helping to expand efforts to identify and protect critical manatee habitats in Florida and neighboring states.

Since 1984, SMC has made it possible for "parents" who join its Adopt-A-Manatee program to follow the life cycle of individual manatees as they migrate, reproduce, get entangled in discarded fishing line, gather at winter refuges—and get hit by powerboats. At present, there are 20 manatees up for adoption at Blue Spring State Park and 5 adoptees available at Homosassa Springs State Wildlife Park. From Howie and Doc to Floyd and Lucille, each of the adoptees has a unique personality and history. Members receive an adoption certificate, a picture of their manatee, a life history, a membership handbook filled with information on manatees, and four newsletters per year. This successful program raises almost $1 million annually to help save the manatees.

To learn more about SMC programs, adopt a manatee, or become a member, call 1-800-432-JOIN.

Where to See Manatees in Florida

THANKS TO THE WONDERFUL MANATEE EXHIBITS THAT HAVE been developed at several museums, zoos, and aquariums throughout Florida, it is now possible to see manatees in captivity year-round. However, if your goal is to see them in the wild, then the best time to visit Florida is from November to the end of March, when cooler water temperatures force the warmth-seeking mammals to congregate at several traditional wintering sites. Manatees often show up in unexpected places during this time, warns the Duval County Manatee Research Project:

"During late October and early November, manatees will be traveling through downtown Jacksonville, perhaps stopping at the warm-water outfalls of Southside and Kennedy Generating Stations. Please exercise extreme caution when boating in these areas. The Intercoastal Waterway will also be more populated with migrating manatees."

Visiting Manatees in Florida

Florida's River Coast

According to travel writer Clive Irving, Florida's River Coast is a special area of the state that stretches north from Aripeka for about 80 miles along the Gulf of Mexico. "It is far less well known than the Everglades, but every bit as richly endowed with wildlife, and more mysterious," says Irving. To the north lies the Lower Suwannee National Wildlife Refuge; to the south, the Chassahowitzka National Wildlife Refuge. In the middle is Cedar Keys National Wildlife Refuge. All three are managed by the U.S. Fish and Wildlife Service.

How fortunate for Florida's manatees and other endangered wildlife that such inaccessible terrain still exists in a state otherwise besieged by waves of retiring senior citizens and a perpetually boating, touring, vacation crowd.

"So far, the River Coast's relative inaccessibility has kept it little changed from the spring of 1513, when Ponce de León passed by on his way up the Gulf coast," adds Irving. "Happily for the land, there is still no coastal road. To see the shoreline you either cruise it by boat or make successive diversions on berm-fringed roads west of the highway."

According to biologist Daniel Hartman, during summer the manatees travel long-established corridors through the complex of sandbars, oyster reefs, and limestone shelves characteristic of this part of the Gulf Coast. The establishment of several wildlife refuges along the west coast has given the endangered animals further protection.

Crystal River

Numerous areas have been protected as manatee refuges in the state of Florida. They are located from Blue Spring State Park on Florida's east coast all the way around the peninsula to Crystal River on the Gulf Coast. Of these, Crystal River National Wildlife Refuge, part of the Chassahowitzka National Wildlife Refuge Complex, is considered one of the most important areas for manatees.

Only two coastal wetland ecosystems remain intact along Florida's entire peninsular shoreline—the Big Bend region along the west coast and the Everglades to the south. South Big Bend encompasses Crystal River and a wide band of coastal marshes, including extensive estuaries that still support abundant seagrass beds—critical habitat needed by manatees. The river's spring-fed 74-degree warmth, ample hydrilla and water hyacinth vegetation, and proximity to the Gulf lure manatees into the river's headwaters at Kings Bay through the fall and winter.

In fact, from mid-November to March, Crystal River is the only place in the world where snorkelers and scuba divers can share underwater time with the endangered West Indian manatees. In 1998 more than 300 manatees passed the winter months here.

They in turn attracted more than 100,000 people, who came in rented boats, wet suits, snorkels, and scuba gear to see them.

Located about 80 miles north of Tampa, the town of Crystal River has several different dive shops that rent equipment and offer snorkeling and diving tours to see the manatees. The town sits on the edge of Kings Bay, named after King Spring, a large sink measuring 75 feet across and 60 feet deep that boils to the surface just south of Banana Island. There are nine islands and several more springs within Kings Bay, all of which are protected as part of the Crystal River National Wildlife Refuge.

Managed by the U.S. Fish and Wildlife Service as part of the Chassahowitzka National Wildlife Refuge Complex, the Crystal River refuge encompasses seven distinct, seasonal manatee sanctuaries within Kings Bays. These no-boat areas are roped off for the wintering manatees from November 15 to March 31. In addition, boat speed zones posted on Crystal River and Kings Bay are enforced by the service from

ABOVE: *Clear water and accessibility have made the Crystal River manatees some of the most photographed animals in the world.*

September 1 to April 30 to protect the migratory animals. Many of the manatees from Crystal River (and Homosassa River) head north to the mouth of the Suwannee River with the return of warmer spring weather.

Homosassa Springs State Wildlife Park

Located just south of Crystal River, 75 miles north of Tampa on the Gulf Coast, Homosassa Springs forms the centerpiece of a picturesque 155-acre wildlife park. According to Marjorie Harris Carr, wife of late naturalist Archie Carr, it is home to "some of Florida's loveliest landscapes, including marshes, swamps, hammocks, and spring runs."

Once operated as an upscale tourist attraction with a floating underwater observatory, Homosassa Springs was purchased by the state of Florida in 1989. Today it is still possible to "walk underwater" in the famous Fish Bowl Spring observatory to watch the mesmerizing movement of 34 different species of fresh- and saltwater fish—along with manatees. The floating observatory, a 168-ton structure built like a ship, was originally launched on rails greased with bananas instead of oil to protect the aquatic wildlife. The beautiful park and unique underwater observatory showcase Florida's native wildlife and endangered species, particularly the West Indian manatee.

In fact, Homosassa Springs State Wildlife Park is the only place manatees can be seen in a natural environment year-round. The park serves as a rehabilitation center for injured manatees, giving them time to acclimatize to a more natural environment before being released back into the wild. Homosassa is also an important refuge for captive-born and orphaned manatees.

As the headwater of the Homosassa River, the 45-foot-deep natural spring pumps millions of gallons of water each hour toward the Gulf of Mexico, located 9 miles away. Miles of nature trails wind throughout the park, giving visitors a chance to experience the wetlands and hammock environments typical of Florida. Park facilities also include a museum and education center, and an observation deck built along the Homosassa River. Interpretive programs about manatees are offered throughout the day by park staff.

Manatee Springs State Park

Located about 60 miles north of Crystal River near Chiefland, Florida, Manatee Springs State Park is surrounded by lush vegetation representative of Florida's unspoiled River Coast. The first-magnitude spring pumps 81,280 gallons of 72-degree-Fahrenheit, crystal-clear water every minute into the Suwannee River, located just 800 to 1,000 feet away.

It was here, on the banks of Manatee Spring in 1773, that William Bartram discovered the skeleton of a manatee. His written account of the event became the first scientific description of the manatee in Florida. Today the "admirable fountain" continues to attract the animals Native Americans once called "big beavers."

However, from November to March, their winter presence is much less consistent than that of the manatee populations found at Crystal River or Blue Spring. The 2,075-acre park has a wheelchair-accessible boardwalk bordering the spring run and excellent nature trails.

Lowry Park Zoo

Located in Tampa, this delightful, 24-acre zoo was ranked as one of the country's three top zoos of its size by the American Association of Zoological Parks and Aquariums. The zoo's Florida Manatee and Aquatic Center combines live animal exhibits with a rehabilitation and research facility engaged in active work with sick and injured manatees. Visitors can see the manatees through 3-inch glass in a 75,000-gallon pool that shows life above and below the water's surface. Educational graphics detail the plight of the West Indian manatee throughout its range and the many conservation projects under way to save the species from extinction. For those interested in the structural design of a manatee, a complete skeleton hangs from the ceiling inside the center near full-size cutouts of the other living sirenians.

ABOVE: *Two metal manatees cavort in a fountain at Tampa's Lowry Park Zoo, where a manatee exhibit is a featured attraction.*

South Florida Museum

Having one of the longest names of any museum, the South Florida Museum, Bishop Planetarium and Parker Manatee Aquarium is located in Bradenton, which is on the south bank of the Manatee River in the heart of Manatee County in southwest Florida. The museum's star attraction is Snooty—the crowd-pleasing captive manatee who has lived at the museum since he was ten months old. Originally called Baby Snoots, the sociable manatee is one of the county's most popular residents and beloved landmarks.

Snooty was born in captivity on July 21, 1948, at the old Miami Aquarium. He is the longest-surviving manatee ever born in captivity. To commemorate his 50th birthday in 1998, the museum created the world's largest birthday card; fed him his favorite strawberries, grapes, and pineapple; and provided him with his first manatee companion. Local-area children also sent Snooty more than 400 birthday cards.

Each year, Snooty entertains about 165,000 museum visitors from his 60,000-gallon tank. He helps teach visitors of all ages about his intelligence and hearing abilities. The famous manatee is also a standard part of classroom curriculum for grades 1 through 3 in Manatee County. Staff presentations about Snooty and other endangered Florida wildlife are given at the museum three times a day.

Earthwatch—Manatee Research Expeditions

"Each day on the boat we sighted manatees," wrote Barbara Colton, an Earthwatch volunteer who helped survey manatees and their seagrass habitats in Florida's Sarasota area in 1996. "Some were grazing on grasses, milling in the shallow waters, cavorting, and some were observed nursing their calves. Each time a sighting took place we all scrambled to our posts, recording the scar formations on diagrams, salinity readings, [and] water and air temperatures, and, of course, the location of each animal was mapped and numbered. Some sightings took as long as 5 hours at a stretch."

Based in Watertown, Massachusetts, Earthwatch is a nonprofit, international organization that supports scientific field research worldwide by matching paying volunteers with scientists engaged in ongoing field research projects. Since its founding in 1971, Earthwatch has mobilized more than 50,000 volunteers, who have contributed over $39 million in research funds to 2,030 projects in 118 countries and 36 states—all while donating 5,963,300 hours of their time as hands-on field research assistants.

In 1998 three Earthwatch teams traveled to Costa Rica to survey the manatees, caimans, and crocodiles of the Tortuguero watershed and to help teach the local children about conservation issues important to their community. That same year, eight additional Earthwatch teams journeyed to Sarasota, Florida, to work with Mote Marine Laboratory scientists as they conducted an annual summertime survey of manatees and their preferred habitats in Sarasota Bay.

To find out what current manatee projects still need volunteers, contact Earthwatch (600 Mount Auburn Street, P.O. Box 9104, Watertown, MA 02272-9104; 617-926-8200), and you too can hear "Muzzles at four o'clock!" as you float over the manatees' shallow seagrass pastures with clipboard and pencil in hand.

Everglades National Park

Manatees find important refuge in the vast, remote waters of Everglades National Park, but they are difficult to see. They do not congregate in large numbers, nor is there a designated public viewing area where they can be observed. Owing to a variety of environmental reasons, few manatees inhabit the Florida Keys or Florida Bay at the southern tip of the state. This creates an informal gap in their distribution between the Gulf of Mexico and the Atlantic Coast, but not a genetic one, as there is a small exchange of animals between both coasts. Manatees frequent the seagrass beds along the park's southwest coast.

Manatee Viewing Center, Riviera Beach

For five decades, Florida Power and Light's Riviera Beach power plant has provided a safe winter haven for manatees. Built in 1946, the plant supplies about 367,000 residences with electricity, recycling an average of 470 million gallons of water drawn from Lake Worth each day for use in the plant's cooling system. Attracted by the warm-water outflow from the plant, manatees have made the Riviera Beach site one of their major winter gathering spots on Florida's east coast. The public is invited to experience this annual wildlife event at the Manatee Viewing Center at the power plant in Riviera

"Manatees are some of the most expensive mammals to feed in captivity. Manatee food can cost $20,000 per animal per year."

൭൭

—SAM WINSLOW,
*Director of Animal Care,
Lowry Park Zoo*

Beach. Open daily from January 2 through February 28, the wheelchair-accessible visitors' center offers audiovisual presentations about manatees as the animals bask outside in their effluvial sauna.

Lee County Manatee Park, Fort Myers

This relatively new park is located next to Florida Power and Light's Fort Myers power plant near the junction of the Caloosahatchee and Orange Rivers. Open year-round, the park offers kayak rentals, picnic shelters, and a nonmotorized boat launch onto the Orange River. During the manatee season from November 1 through March 31, daily manatee presentations are given by volunteer naturalists. The park includes three manatee viewing areas with educational kiosks and a visitors' center and gift shop. Pets, bikes, and skates are not allowed.

Big Bend Station Manatee Viewing Center

Each winter, manatees gather in the artificially warmed discharge canal below Tampa Electric Company's Big Bend Station. To make it possible for the public to enjoy this wildlife spectacle, the electric company built the special Manatee Viewing Center. Open from November to April, the center includes an observation platform above the canal, a tidal flat walkway, and an Environmental Education Building that features full-size murals, underwater photographs, a manatee skeleton, and an 11½-foot fiberglass manatee sculpture. In 1986 the state of Florida designated the plant's discharge canal a manatee sanctuary, which means that boating, fishing, swimming, and feeding manatees are not permitted.

> "I was able to meet, briefly but pleasurably, what may be the gentlest creature on earth—the manatee. . . . Seen full-face, the manatee is so homely of visage, its expression one of such innocence as to be utterly beguiling."
>
> —FAITH MCNULTY, *from* The Wildlife Stories of Faith McNulty

Miami Seaquarium®

Since the early 1970s, the Miami Seaquarium has participated in the recovery and rehabilitation of dozens of manatees. It also houses the most prolific manatee breeding colony anywhere in the United States. Although the Seaquarium's rehabilitation area is closed to the public, visitors can view a half dozen or more manatees featured in the park's 90,000-gallon Celebrity Pool. The resident manatees can be seen from above and through an underwater viewing area. Manatee education programs are presented at poolside three times each day by aquarium staff.

The Living Seas, Walt Disney World Resort, Epcot

Located at Epcot, *The Living Seas* is Walt Disney World's center for marine science and conservation. The center's 6-million-gallon aquarium, one of the largest in the world, is home to more than 2,700 fish, plus sharks, sea turtles, bottle-nosed dolphins—and

ABOVE: *Manatees float protected and content at the Miami Seaquarium.*

manatees. Visited by millions of people, *The Living Seas* works as a partner with other local conservation organizations in efforts to rescue, rehabilitate, and eventually return injured manatees to the wild.

SeaWorld Orlando

In 1993, SeaWorld Orlando opened its popular exhibit "Manatees: The Last Generation?" Combining an omnidome movie presentation with staff talks and educational graphics, the two-story exhibit guides visitors through a 300,000-gallon manatee habitat that has been designed to look like a lush tropical lagoon. A 126-foot-long acrylic panel makes it possible to get a good underwater view of the manatees in the exhibit as they cruise, feed, doze, and tag along after staff scuba divers. The manatees can also be viewed from an observation area above the water. Touch-screen kiosks are positioned throughout the exhibit so visitors can ask and answer questions about the manatee's lifestyle while actually viewing the animals.

Blue Spring State Park

Blue Spring State Park, located 2 miles from Orange City near Deland, is a beautiful place to visit, to swim, picnic, or just enjoy the scenery. For Florida's endangered manatees, the park provides winter habitat that is critical for their survival. From November

LEFT: *Two plump manatees feed on lettuce at SeaWorld Orlando, often giving visitors their first glimpse of these plant-eating marine mammals.*

"Much of the early interest in wildlife conservation grew out of a desire to save some of the world's most spectacular mammals, and to some extent, these so-called charismatic megavertebrates are still the best vehicles for conveying the entire issue of conservation to the public. They really are our flagship species, both here in the United States and in the developing countries."

〜

—RUSSELL A. MITTERMEIER, *President, Conservation International*

to March, 80 to 90 manatees congregate at Blue Spring State Park. A self-guided, ½-mile boardwalk meanders through lush hammock vegetation as it hugs the length of the spring run from the picturesque Blue Spring boil to the St. Johns River. Observation platforms built on stilts over the water make it easy to view the park's wintering manatees from land as they rest submerged on the bottom of the spring run, nurse their calves, play, and expel their voluminous breaths of air in loud, heavy sighs at the surface. Powerboats are not allowed in the spring run at any time, and a "Slow Speed–Idle Zone" has been established a mile above and below the run on the St. Johns River. Swimming is permitted in the park, but only in an area far away from the manatees.

Merritt Island National Wildlife Refuge

After the Kennedy Space Center was established in 1961, NASA invited the U.S. Fish and Wildlife Service to manage the surrounding buffer lands that were not directly needed for the space program. In 1963 the Merritt Island National Wildlife Refuge was created as a sanctuary for wintering waterfowl. Twelve years later, the National Park Service established the adjacent Canaveral National Seashore to preserve the primitive barrier beach and make parts of it accessible to the public.

RIGHT: *Schoolchildren point out the ghostly gray shapes of manatees camouflaged at Blue Spring State Park. Public education plays an important role in the ongoing conservation of these endangered animals.*

Considered a barrier island, Merritt Island is surrounded by the Indian River to the west and the Mosquito Lagoon, Atlantic Ocean, and Banana River to the east. About 13,000 acres of the refuge are considered a manatee sanctuary, including most of the Banana River, where motorized boats have been prohibited since 1990. The ban proved effective, as more than 400 manatees were counted here in the spring of 1993, and the numbers have increased each year. In addition to a manatee watch overlooking Mosquito Lagoon, and glimpses of wintering manatees in the Indian River, refuge visitors can look for manatees in the Banana River—if they are willing to use a nonmotorized boat to quietly paddle, sail, or row among them.

Fort Pierce Manatee Observatory

The Fort Pierce Manatee Observation and Education Center is located on Indian River Drive near the Fort Pierce Utilities Authority (FPUA) power plant. Managed by the FPUA, the center is open six days a week from November to April, when the power plant's warm-water outflow into Moore's Creek has attracted up to sixty wintering manatees. A covered walkway and tower offer visitors excellent views of the manatees in their natural habitat, while the center's exhibit area explains the importance of protecting the fragile ecosystem along Florida's famous Treasure Coast.

What You Can Do to Help Save the Manatees

People are by far the greatest threat to manatees. Directly and indirectly, we are responsible for the deaths of many manatees each year. Aside from giving the animals plenty of room, here are a few suggestions from the Duval County Manatee Research Project on how to pass gently through manatee country.

- If you own a boat, obey the posted speed limits and keep your vessel at least 50 feet away from any manatee you spot. Stay in deep water, away from shorelines and grassbeds. Avoid passing directly over submerged animals. Wear polarized sunglasses for greater visibility into water.
- If you dive, look, but do not touch the manatees. Do not chase or follow manatees that are leaving your areas. Never separate a cow and calf, and stay out of manatee refuge areas. These areas are clearly marked and are off-limits to people.
- If you fish, do not discard monofilament line, hooks, or other litter into the water. Not only is it unlawful, it can cause serious injury or death to the manatees.
- Do not feed manatees, or "water" them with your dockside hose. When wild animals lose their natural fear of humans, they become more vulnerable to injury or death.
- If you see a dead or injured manatee, or anyone harassing a manatee, call the Florida Marine Patrol's Manatee Hot Line at 1-800-DIAL-FMP.

"Biodiversity is out there in nature, everywhere you look, an enormous cornucopia of wild and cultivated species, diverse in form and function, with beauty and usefulness beyond the wildest imagination."

—HUGH H. ILTIS,
Emeritus Director,
University of Wisconsin
Herbarium

Bibliography

∾

Allsopp, W.H.L. 1969. Aquatic weed control by manatees—its prospects and problems. In L.E. Obeng (ed.), *Man-Made Lakes: The Accra Symposium,* pp. 344–51. Accra: Ghana Universities Press.

Anderson, P.K. 1986. Dugongs of Shark Bay, Australia—Seasonal migration, water temperature, and forage. *National Geographic Research* 2:473–90.

Baden, D., K.S. Rein, J. Delgado-Arias, P.L. Whitney, S. Wright, and G. Bossart. 1998. Red Alert: Brevetoxins accumulate in manatee phagocytic cells, inhibit intracellular cathepsin enzymes, lead to cell apoptosis and animal death. *Toxicologic Pathology,* Vol. 26, 276–82.

Barry, D. 1998. Manatee love. *The Miami Herald,* April 26.

Bartram, W. 1988. *Travels Through North and South Carolina, Georgia, East and West Florida.* New York: Penguin.

Bates, H.W. 1875. *The Naturalist on the River Amazons.* New York: E.P. Dutton & Co.

Beck, C. A., and N. B. Barros. 1991. The impact of debris on the Florida manatee. *Marine Pollution Bulletin* 22(10):508–10.

Belleville, B. 1997. "Another roadside attraction: Beyond billboards; glimpses of eternity." *Sierra,* Sept./Oct.

Best, R.C. 1983. Apparent dry-season fasting in Amazonian manatees (Mammalia: Sirenia). *Biotropica* 15:61–64.

Bloch, Nini. 1993. The last mermaids. *Earthwatch* 12(7):17–23.

Block, N. 1993. The Last Mermaids. *Earthwatch,* Nov./Dec.

Bolt, B. 1998. *Merritt Island National Wildlife Refuge.* Albuquerque, NM: Public Lands Interpretive Association.

Bonde, R.K. 1993. Manatees in Florida: a personal perspective. *Whalewatcher* 27(1):16–18.

Bonde, R.K., and C. A. Beck. 1990. How the Florida manatees fare today. *Whalewatcher* 24(1):8–9.

Brandes, K. (ed.). 1974. *Vanishing Species.* New York: TIME-LIFE Books.

Caras, R. 1970. *Vanishing Wildlife.* Richmond, Va.: Westover Publishing Co.

Carr, Archie. 1994. *A Naturalist in Florida: A Celebration of Eden.* New Haven, Conn.: Yale University Press.

Carrington, R. 1957. *Mermaids and Mastodons: A Book of Natural & Unnatural History.* London: Chatto and Windus.

Carson, R. 1973. *Silent Spring.* Boston: Houghton Mifflin Company.

Cousteau, J.M. 1991. Eco-War in the Gulf. *Calypso Log,* April 3.

Deutsch, C.J., R.K. Bonde, and J.P. Reid. 1998. Radio-tracking manatees from land and space: Tag design, implementation, and lessons learned from long-term study. *MTS* 32(1):18–29.

Diamond, J. 1992. *The Third Chimpanzee: The Evolution and Future of the Human Animal.* New York: HarperCollins Publishers.

Dietz, T. 1992. *The Call of the Siren: Manatees and Dugongs.* Golden, Colo.: Fulcrum Publishing.

Domning, D.P. 1981. Manatees of the Amazon. *Sea Frontiers* 27:18–23.

———. 1982. Commercial exploitation of manatees *(Trichechus)* in Brazil c. 1785–1973. *Biological Conservation* 22:101–26.

———. 1982. Evolution of manatees: A speculative history. *Journal of Paleontology* 56:599–619.

Domning, D.P. (ed.), 1997. *Sirenews.* Newsletter of the IUCN/SSC Sirenian Specialist Group. No. 27 and No. 28.

Domning, D.P., and V. DeBuffrenil. 1991. Hydrostatis in the Sirenia: quantitative data and functional interpretations. *Marine Mammal Science* 7:331–68.

Gerstein, E.R. 1994. The manatee mind: discrimination training for sensory perception testing of West Indian manatees *(Trichechus manatus). Marine Mammals: Public Display and Research.* Vol. 1, pp. 10–21.

———. (in review) Discrimination of aqueous solutions by West Indian manatees: notes on taste and chemoreception.

Gerstein, E.R., and J.E. Blue. 1996. Near surface acoustic properties of manatee habitats. Tech Report: DACW39-92R-0112, U.S. Army Corps of Engineers.

Gerstein, E.R., L.A. Gerstein, S. Forsythe, and J.E. Blue (in press). The underwater audiogram of the West Indian manatee (*Trichechus manatus*). *Journal of the Acoustical Society of America*.

Goodwin, G. 1954. *The Animal Kingdom*. New York: Greystone Press.

Grzimek, B. 1972. *Grzimek's Animal Encyclopedia*. Vol. 12. New York: Van Nostrand Reinhold Company.

Hall, A.J. 1984. Man and manatee: Can we live together? *National Geographic* 166:400–413.

Hartman, D.S. 1969. Florida's manatees, mermaids in peril. *National Geographic* 136:342–53.

————. 1979. *Ecology and behavior of the manatee* (Trichechus manatus) *in Florida*. American Society of Mammalogists, Special Pub. no. 5.

Holland, J. 1971. *The Amazon*. Cranbury, N.J.: A.S. Barnes and Co., Inc.

Hotta, A. 1998. *Manatee*. San Francisco: Chronicle Books.

Irvine, A.B. 1983. Manatee metabolism and its influence in distribution in Florida. *Biological Conservation* 25:315–34.

Irving, C. 1992. Florida, Low on the water. *Condé Nast Traveler,* May.

Kaplan, S. 1989. Orlando Without Mickey. *Travel-Holiday,* September.

Kensinger, G. 1977. *Strangest Creatures of the World*. New York: Bantam Books.

Ketten, D.R., D.K. Odell, and D.P. Domning. 1992. Structure, function, and adaptation of the manatee ear. In J. Thomas et al. (eds.), *Marine mammal sensory systems,* pp. 77–95. New York: Plenum Press.

Kumin, M. 1997. *Maxine Kumin: Selected Poems, 1960–1990*. New York: W.W. Norton Co.

Lenihan, D. J. 1996. Raptures of the Deep. *Natural History,* November.

Lydekker, R. 1894. *The Royal Natural History*. London: Frederick Warne & Co.

Macdonald, D. (ed.). 1984. *The Encyclopedia of Mammals*. New York: Facts on File.

MacLaren, J.P. 1967. Manatees as a naturalistic biological mosquito control method. *Mosquito News* 27 (3):387–93.

Marsh, H. 1988. An ecological basis for dugong conservation in Australia. In M.L. Augee (ed.), *Marine Mammals of Australasia: Field Biology and Captive Management,* pp. 9–21. Sydney, Australia: Royal Zoological Society of New South Wales.

Marsh, H., G. E. Heinsohn, and L.M. Marsh. 1984. Breeding cycle, life history and population dynamics of the dugong, *Dugong dugon* (Sirenia: Dugongidae). *Australian Journal of Zoology* 32:767–88.

Marsh, H., and L.W. Lefebvre. 1994. Sirenian status and conservation efforts. *Aquatic Mammals* 20(3):155–70.

Marshall, C.D., G.D. Huth, V.M. Edmonds, D.L. Halin, and R.L. Reep. 1998. Prehensile use of perioral bristles during feeding and associated behaviors of the Florida manatee (*Trichechus manatus latirostris*). *Marine Mammal Science* 14(2):274–89.

McClung, R. 1978. *Hunted Mammals of the Sea*. New York: William Morrow and Company.

McNulty, F. 1980. *The Wildlife Stories of Faith McNulty*. Garden City, N.Y.: Doubleday.

Montgomery, G.G., R.C. Best, and M. Yamakoshi. 1981. A radio-tracking study of the Amazonian manatee *Trichechus inunguis* (Mammalia: Sirenia). *Biotropica* 13:81–85.

Moore, J. 1957. *Observations of Manatees in Aggregations*. American Museum of Natural History Novitates, no. 1811.

O'Hara, J. 1967. Invertebrates found in water hyacinth mats. *Quarterly Journal of the Florida Academy of Science* 30:73–80.

O'Keefe, M.T. 1993. *Manatees: Our Vanishing Mermaids*. Lakeland, Fla.: Larsen's Outdoor Publishing.

O'Shea, T.J. 1994. Manatees. *Scientific American* 271(1): 66–72.

O'Shea, T.J., B.B. Ackerman, and H.F. Percival (eds.). 1995. *Population Biology of the Florida Manatee* (Trichechus manatus latirostris). National Biological Service, Information and Technology Report 1.

O'Shea, T.J., and R.L. Reep. 1990. Encephalization quotients and life-history traits in the *Sirenia. Journal of Mammalogy* 71:534–43.

O'Shea, T.J., G.B. Rathbun, R.K. Bonde, C.D. Buergelt, and D.K. Odell. 1991. An epizootic of Florida manatees associated with a dinoflagellate bloom. *Marine Mammal Science* 7:165–79.

O'Shea, T.J., and C.A. Salisbury. 1991. Belize—a last stronghold for manatees in the Caribbean. *Oryx* 25(3):156–64.

Packard, J.M., R.K. Frohlich, J.E. Reynolds III, and J.R. Wilcox. 1989. Manatee response to interruption of a thermal effluent. *Journal of Wildlife Management* 53(3):692–700.

Packard, J.M., G.B. Rathbun, and D.P. Domning. 1984. Sea cows and manatees. In D. Macdonald (ed.), *The Encyclopedia of Mammals,* pp. 291–303. New York: Facts on File.

Powell, J.A. 1978. Evidence of carnivory in manatees *(Trichechus manatus). Journal of Mammalogy* 59:442.

Rathbun, G.B., J.P. Reid, and G. Carowan. 1990. Distribution and movement patterns of manatees *(Trichechus manatus)* in northwestern peninsular Florida. *Florida Marine Research Publications* 48:1–33.

Ray, C.E., and D.P. Domning. 1986. Manatees and Genocide. *Marine Mammal Science* 2(1):77–78.

Reeves, R.R., B.S. Stewart, and S. Leatherwood. 1992. *The Sierra Club Handbook of Seals and Sirenians.* San Francisco: Sierra Club Books.

Reeves, R.R., D. Tuboku-Metzger, and R.A. Kapindi. 1988. Distribution and exploitation of manatees in Sierra Leone. *Oryx* 22:75–84.

Reynolds, J.E., III. 1979. The semisocial manatee. *Natural History* 88:44–53.

———. 1981. Aspects of the social behavior and herd structure of a semi-isolated colony of West Indian manatees, *Trichechus manatus. Mammalia* 45:431–51.

Reynolds, J.E., III, and D.K. Odell. 1991. *Manatees and Dugongs.* New York: Facts on File.

Reynolds, J.E., III, and J.R. Wilcox. 1986. Distribution and abundance of the West Indian manatee *Trichechus manatus* around selected Florida power plants following winter cold fronts: 1984–1985. *Biological Conservation* 38:103–13.

Scheffer, V.B. 1972. The weight of the Steller sea cow. *Journal of Mammalogy* 53(4):912–14.

Shoumatoff, A. 1986. *The Rivers Amazon.* San Francisco: Sierra Club Books.

Smith, A., and H. Marsh. 1990. Management of traditional hunting of dugongs [*Dugong dugon* (Muller, 1976)] in the northern Great Barrier Reef, Australia. *Environmental Management* 14:47–55.

Stejneger, L. 1887. How the great northern sea-cow *(Rytina)* became exterminated. *American Naturalist* 21:1047–54.

———. 1936. *Georg Wilhelm Steller: The Pioneer of Alaskan Natural History.* Cambridge, Mass.: Harvard University Press.

Steller, G.W. (W. Miller and J. E. Miller, trans.). 1899. The beasts of the sea. In D.S. Jordan, The fur seals and fur-seal islands of the North Pacific Ocean. Government Printing Office, Washington, D.C., Part 3, pp. 179–218.

Stolenburg, W. 1991. The fragment connection. *Nature Conservancy,* July/August.

Timm, R.M., L. Albuja V., and B.L. Clauson. 1986. Ecology, distribution, harvest, and conservation of the Amazonian manatee *Trichechus inunguis* in Ecuador. *Biotropica* 18:150–56.

Unterbrink, M. 1984. *Manatees: Gentle Giants in Peril.* St. Petersburg, Fla.: Great Outdoors Publishing Co.

U.S. Fish and Wildlife Service. 1995. Florida Manatee Recovery Plan, Second Revision. Atlanta, Ga.: U.S. Fish and Wildlife Service.

Vallee, J. 1994. Manatees and boats—a collision course. *Florida Naturalist* 67:15–17.

Van Doren, M. 1976. *Travels of William Bartram.* New York: Dover Publications.

Van Meter, V.B. 1989. *The West Indian Manatee in Florida.* Miami, Fla.: Florida Power and Light Company.

Vietmeyer, N. 1974. The endangered but useful manatee. *Smithsonian,* December.

Walters, M.J. 1985. Marvelous, magnificent manatees. *Reader's Digest,* August.

Williams, J. 1988. Swamp Song. *Condé Nast Traveler,* April.

Wilson, E.O. (ed.). 1988. *Biodiversity.* Washington, D.C.: National Academy Press.

Wrangham, R., and D. Peterson. 1996. *The Demonic Male: Apes and the Origins of Human Violence.* Boston: Houghton-Mifflin.

Zeiller, W. 1992. *Introducing the Manatee.* Gainesville, Fla.: University Press of Florida.

Index

INDEX

Index

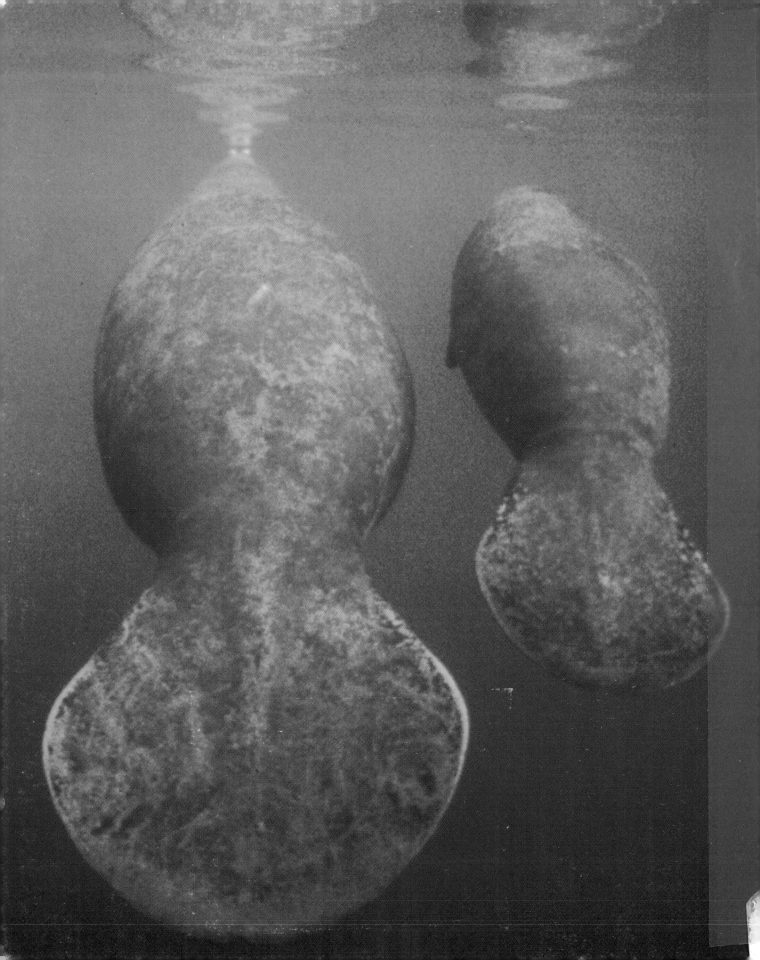